MORANDI

RIZZOLI
NEW YORK

Coordination: Domenico Pertocoli
English language translation: A&P Editing, Andrew Ellis
Composition: Thoth Style, Milan
Printed and bound in Italy by: Leva Arti Grafiche, Sesto S. Giovanni (Milan)

This book was originally published as a catalogue for the exhibition held at the Hôtel de Ville in Paris, 12 June - 20 August 1987, organized in association with the Bologna City Council at the suggestion of Mazzotta publishers, Milan.
We would like to thank the following individuals and organizations for their permission to reproduce works of Morandi: Anna and Maria Teresa Morandi, Bologna; the Galleria Comunale d'Arte Moderna, Bologna; Lamberto Vitali, Milan; Laura Mattioli, Milan; the Pinacoteca di Brera, Milan; the Civico Museo d'Arte Contemporanea, Milan; Franco Fabbi, Modena; Salvatore Italo Magliano, Milan; Gabriele Mazzotta, Milan; Efrem Salvaterra, Modena; Efrem Tavoni, Sasso Marconi; Antonello Trombadori, Rome; Massimo Di Carlo, Verona; Achille Maramotti, Albinea; Carlo Zucchini, Bologna; the Musée National d'Art Moderne, Centre Georges Pompidou, Paris; Marie-France Latarjet, Paris; Marilena Pasquali, Bologna; Franco Solmi, Bologna.

First published in the United States of America in 1988 by
RIZZOLI INTERNATIONAL PUBLICATIONS, INC.
597 Fifth Avenue, New York, NY 10017

ISBN 0-8478-0930-7
LC 87-43274

Contents

5   The Art of Morandi - *Franco Solmi*

19   Giorgio Morandi - A Secret World - *Lamberto Vitali*

23   Paintings

79   Watercolors

89   Drawings

105   Etchings

139   Biography - *Marilena Pasquali*

146   Select Bibliography

148   Exhibitions - *Marilena Pasquali*

155   Catalogue of Works

Giorgio Morandi (photo by Herbert List).

The Art of Morandi

Franco Solmi

"Morandi's painting style unfolds with time, tacitly faithful to itself and yet forever changing, through variations that are almost imperceptible at the apex but increasingly conspicuous towards the base — perhaps it is like an 'olive branch' in the midst of modern painting?" It is hard to say what this somewhat prophetic statement of Cesare Brandi's may mean to today's chaotic world of distressing and turbulent images. There is certainly a growing number of scholars in both Europe and America who are attracted by Morandi's cogent yet discreet appeal and interested in assessing his contribution to the art world. Morandi's emblematic images seem to dwell both at the very core and at the extreme borders of an impalpable sense of inner transgression, tokens of an inchoate but measured rejection of the system of codes which have come to threaten the innermost substance of the highly individual style of the artist, the raw structure of his art, the apprehensive magma in which the innate partiality of language dissolves, and finds resolve, in the work of art, with its reserve of poetry. If a painting style were truly distinctive and faithful to the individual personality of an artist, it could prove to be one of the rare instruments of resistance against the infinite conformities that inform the imagery of the electronic age, including its esthetics. It is a matter of transgression and resistance, not absolute negation, because art — and the art of Giorgio Morandi in particular — can exist and can endure both within and without the flow of events, but only in order to establish its own modernity, its inescapable present.

The marvel of Morandi's work lies in the apparently irreconcilable tensions and formal dialectics that are simultaneously underscored and held in check through the integrity of a highly personal style that is at the same time both restive and firm. He succeeded in upholding this dynamic more limpidly perhaps than any other artist of this century. His ability to apprehend was total. He had adopted Pascal as "his own," and I believe he remained faithful to one of the philosopher's fondest thoughts, as he always painted, drew, and engraved with the awareness that "you cannot demonstrate your own greatness by remaining at one extreme, but by reaching out to both extremes at the same time, and filling the intermediate space." Such a condition is impossible for a human being to maintain, and is always at risk. When it is achieved at all, it is only through artistic expression, and the condition Morandi cultivated is without doubt common to all periods of history: it is a condition tied to one of the most persistent aspirations of Man (and not least of the artist) — that is, to express himself in his totality, to *create*. Perhaps this is a cultural illusion of an old and unburied Europe.

Although his work is descended from a legacy of implacable traditions, Morandi represented the height of modernity for the Italians. The problem in Morandi's work of either being present and participative, or of being detached — of being with the times or completely anachronistic — is an issue that keeps coming back unchanged, like some dilemma that pursues us — almost, even, like a discourse on things we have loved, or long despised, but which exercises both a subtle attraction and a poison on the mind. The metaphor of the olive branch that highlights the closing lines of an essay of extraordinary lucidity and critical rigor, seems to foreshadow the return of artists to the "opus," to painting created with classical artistic methods, and it may well help us discover unresolved questions and put forward some completely new ones in the meantime.

The quote from Brandi is taken from the second edition of the volume *Morandi* published by Le Monnier in 1952, a year in which banal decrees on the demise of brush painting were circulating in Italy, amid nagging rumors regarding the death of Art. It signalled a lengthy season of fervent enthusiasm and superficial confidence, a mood to which Morandi as usual remained quite alien, though by no means indifferent. In fact his late works betray a fresh murmur of restlessness that seems to hint at a secret and sometimes anguished participation, almost as if the artist were bracing himself against the mounting disintegration and the implacable sublimations of Conceptual Art. Artistic expression was increasingly geared to *effect* and to the ritual of *performance*, and the humble and tenacious painting of Giorgio Morandi seemed to recede further and further into the past — for almost twenty years after the death of the artist most critics fell regularly into ritual "noble celebrations" of Morandi's work, which, despite inspiring an occasional prominent study, seemed unable to penetrate the living dialectic of the process of achieving true modernity. Moreover, the times and generations had changed. The young were caught in a sea of fresh formal and linguistic currents in which the ailing European culture was foundering. The classical technique of "brush painting" seemed so removed and inaccessible, it was dethroned and swept aside in the aggressive neo-avant-garde climate. Or alternatively, it was held to exist in a kind of remote dimension of its own, out of reach of the contaminations of international style. In both cases the outcome was the same, and was an echo of a long-standing autarchy, at once humble and proud, that had been fueled for several decades — not by Morandi himself but by a grass-roots Morandian following, and by an analysis that was predominantly idealistic and merely confirmed the shortcomings of its own critical tools by seeking relief in the survivors of "absolute" art. And what better refuge than the Morandian oasis, in which poetry (still used as a synonym for pictorial quality) could be found in its most certain and eminent form? What was being advocated as the Morandian absolute was dressed up with outdated and even esoteric virtues, and verged on a form of abstract morality. The full gamut of values that had already tainted the first monograph on Giorgio Morandi by Arnaldo Beccaria, namely Intuition, Purity, Universality, and Interiority, appeared again, in an even more elaborate and refined form, in the volume published by Cesare Gnudi in 1946. This approach was to become a standard in the post-war years, and naturally filtered through into the studies of Brandi and Lamberto Vitali. While in their hands it was subtly enriched, in substance it remained largely intact, and was carried onto the pages of Francesco Arcangeli, though not without some basic transgressions. Beccaria was somewhat blinded by what he defined as "incense burned on the altar of silence," which he had breathed like a drug in the paintings of his friend; consequently Morandi's most faithful critic did nothing but seek out new motifs for a beautiful and mystical dream.

In his first draft of the essay, Brandi had written that in his painting the Bolognese master "rose to the very sublimation of escape, resonant with contemplation." When it came to Francesco Arcangeli however, he was more set on getting past this awkward barrier of abstract perfections in order to restore physical presence to the things and objects, and saw a real and solid world where others had only seen the sublime. "Morandi's ability to express this extraordinary calm and moral fullness," wrote Arcangeli in 1950, "will push his art far beyond the limits imposed on it by the subject matter, and he will acquire universal value during this century." But we know that the universality of Morandi does not lie simply in the tranquility and moral fullness he expressed, but in the cloistered disquiet, in the almost unbearable tensions which are not infrequently animated by a spark of drama. This I believe applies equally to all his paintings, including those from the metaphysical period. The work of the recluse from Via Fondazza symbolizes a modern form of universality, one that still ranks amongst the highest human aspirations, but which has been irreparably threatened, the only universality that we are capable of imagining in this century: that is, the translation of things into images. In his book of 1964 Arcangeli made a bold attempt at removing a few stones from the Morandian "Olympus," hoping to pry open the gates of the stronghold in which the works of the artist were being constantly stored away, but he failed. He had tried unsuccessfully to equate Morandi's art with an ultimate and almost desperate naturalism, and to link it to the new frontier of the Informal. Morandi himself disclaimed the book, and this quite understandably helped to accentuate the critical isolation of an artist who stood way outside the arena of polemics, but who was also emarginated from the more interesting aspects of debate extolled by the critics in general and which so attracted the front-line generations of the 1960s and 1970s. Given the current character of retrospectives, unabashed anachronisms, and frequently bold revivals of past art forms, one can only hope that Morandi's art will not simply be re-appraised out of boredom with the present.

Even critics devoted to philological analysis have found in Morandi's painting, with its wealth of secret, mysterious and occasionally impregnable resonances, a source of enigmatic images that evoke a literary sense, bordering on prophecy.

On the occasion of the inaugural lecture of the art history course at Bologna University for the academic year 1934/35, Roberto Longhi wound up his fundamental and painstaking examination of the crucial moments of Bolognese painting — from the ''Trecentisti'' to the very last ''focherello carraccesco,'' or nineteenth-century painters in the Carracci line — by saying to an astonished audience ''It is no coincidence that one of the finest living painters in Italy, Giorgio Morandi, despite his navigating among the more treacherous areas of modern painting, has nonetheless steered his course with mindful slowness, with his love of study, so much so that his art seems to emerge as a new genus. In today's world, the tumult of images conspires to suffocate the slow silences and meditations of art, so that the 'love of study' seems unable to withstand the blast of infinite and cruel diversions; that presence which remains faithful to a highly individual way of feeling and of painting seems to become strangely familiar to us, to offer us an unimaginable certainty, a standard that not only resists, but, being new, asserts itself.''

These words of Longhi's not only prompted the beginnings of a ''Morandi question,'' but also of an official history and the legend of Via Fondazza. Both the history and the legend are quite unique, and each one is co-witness and essential to the other, brimming with unresolved conjecture, with details so simple that they appear at once both true and false.

It was the singular nature of this background that contributed to the birth of the legend, and certainly the legend in turn affected the history. In truth, history and legend — on the one hand the definable and profound participation in the concrete life of art, and on the other, the cloistered withdrawal from the fury of debate — concur to provide a credible image of the man and the painter. He was undoubtedly an exception as he managed to fuse an eminently human metaphysics, a vital sense of sacred and profane, of mystical exaltation and of everyday domesticity in a life with no miracles to speak of. This is sufficient to justify a legend, and serves equally as a history, if we are to avoid reciting a mere list of facts that convey little of the mystery that always accompanies human activity, and to an even greater extent artistic activity.

I would by no means deny the legitimacy and significance of the ''mystery'' of Morandi's genius, nor the work of those who have tenaciously tried to spread it. Men and things, even those that belong to art, are without doubt what they appear to be, and each of us must naturally choose his own prototype for making judgments. We might say however that discussions on the Bolognese painter are rarely dispassionate. This artist was party in one way or another throughout his life to the events that took place in an Italy which had been a province of Europe for over half a century, and he was obliged to suffer misunderstanding and negative criticism, especially when he had to disavow the imaginative praise of those who interpreted his works as a tranquil progression towards increasingly perfect formal achievements — almost the progress of an intellect capable of creating its own time and space, completely outside any cultural influence. This misapprehension was nearly always the result of a failure to grasp the dispersions and personal desperation of the artist, to appreciate his uncertainties and disquiet, to distinguish the unsuccessful canvases from the master-works. Nevertheless, all these attempts at interpretation have in one way or another managed to penetrate some aspect of Morandi's world of art and culture. After each enquiry, the picture has appeared a little clearer, and a new critical dimension has come to the surface. This is a sign that the Morandi phenomenon is a highly complex one, and that the many roads tried so far have not yet reached the heart of the problem. For this reason, Morandi remains, as I have said, one of the most intriguing problems of art of this century.

The deepest undercurrents of the painting of Giorgio Morandi bear the inescapable imprint of French artistic culture, especially that which developed around the mold of Cézanne — the master the young Bolognese artist chose from the outset, and whom, we might add, he was to revere all his life. Bologna at the start of the century was still very much under Papal influence, and as such was irreparably provincial. It is hard to imagine the effect on society of the truly European intuition of this group of young people, who had received their ideas of Cézanne and the Impressionists through the writings of Ardengo Soffici in the Florentine magazine *La Voce*, without even having seen the works, which were to become a decisive point of reference for them, except in black and white reproductions. Osvaldo Licini, Mario Bacchelli, Giacomo Vespignani, and Severo Pozzati (who made a name for himself in France as a poster designer under the name of Sepo) were Morandi's companions in adventure and discovery, the same ones who had quickly chosen Rousseau, Braque, Picasso, and Derain as their mentors. The now famous exhibition at the Hotel Baglioni in Bologna held by the group on 21 May 1914 brought about the encounter with the wild acolytes of Emilio Marinetti who had founded the magazine *Lacerba*.

It is here that we find the very first reference to Morandi. This extemporaneous exhibition caused quite a stir in the rather somnolent Bologna of the day. Together with a handful of drawings and several versions of *Still Life of Mirrors* with a decisive Futurist bent to them, Morandi exhibited two paintings — the *Landscape* of 1911 (Vitali Collection), and the *Portrait of the Artist's Sister* Dina which until Morandi's death was thought to have been lost. Writing on the *Landscape* Lamberto Vitali commented that "it is the handiwork of an accomplished and unhesitant artist in possession of a language that is destined to grow steadily more defined, without altering its basic terms." In accord with most scholars of Morandi, Brandi considers this painting a point of departure for every later step in the artist's research. "The first step of this path," wrote Brandi, "was made in 1911, and can be traced to a landscape painting of that year — a small canvas in which the painter, who was only twenty-one at the time, used a few clustered dense strokes to create a vision of a village that was neither idyllic nor welcoming, and whose horizon, swelling like a wave that is about to break, pushes up against a vast sky with no respite.'' The distribution of the masses in this painting is indeed leaden and spare, and the meager use of color relies largely on dim gray tones, silvery green, and the merest hint of blue. It is a studio painting, without doubt, and its composition is based on the methods Morandi used later for his still lifes. There is nothing ''natural'' or naturalistic in that compact enclosing of things and their suspension in a still and immemorial time. This tribute to nature lives on an ideal level. A veil of ancient gray powder casts a weak light on this landscape, which already betrays a metaphysical atmosphere, locking it in its static truth. ''This canvas of mine is direct, it does not vacillate, it is true, dense, and full...'' Cézanne would surely have recognized something of himself in it.

Before executing this landscape, Morandi had painted a little *Tree-lined Avenue* with a slightly Impressionistic tone, and one *Snowfall*, which also feeds on a dense light that lends structure to the whole. The painting was put on show for the first time in the exhibition ''Morandi e il suo tempo'' held in Bologna through the winter season from 1985 to 1986. But this find in no way invalidates what has been said of the Vitali Collection *Landscape*, in which the colors seem to turn to ash — an achievement which thrusts Morandi from his provincial backwater into the mainstream of the European avant-garde. Brandi quite correctly distinguishes Morandi from the followers of Cézanne, who, he observed ''were largely ensnared in that halo of blue on the trees and hills... Morandi did not know the colors of Cézanne's paintings and managed to avoid this pitfall, unlike Picasso and Matisse, who some years earlier had committed themselves to ensuring the new directions of modern art based on the legacy of Cézanne.''

The *Portrait of the Artist's Sister* poses a problem, so far unresolved by the Italian critics. We do not know what the young painter can have seen of Derain's work back in 1912, when none of the French master's works had ever appeared in Italian magazines. Soffici, who traveled frequently between Florence and Paris bringing back news for publication in *La Voce* and *Lacerba*, had at one point referred to Derain as one of the artists who opposed Fauvism, following instead the model of Picasso and Braque. A *Self-Portrait* by Licini dated 1913, with its harsh compact structure and rough material resembling plaster is strikingly similar in expression to the *Portrait of the Artist's Sister* painted by the young Morandi. Licini was thirsty for news from Paris where he had relatives who sent him photographs, books, and essays on art in France. Soffici for his part was an artist whose work was always consistent with his writings, and his paintings allude not only to Braque and Picasso, but also to Derain, especially in the *Bathers* series; it was from him that Morandi evidently took inspiration when he painted his rare *Nudes*, which bear the unmistakable imprint of Cézanne's *Bathers*.

The two 1913 pictures *Snowscape* and the Jucker Collection *Landscape*, which both have the theme of a central tree, and the *Landscape* (Private collection, Bologna) announce the shift from lateral Cubism towards the style used in the still lifes of 1914 (including the highly unusual large painting now in the Centre Pompidou, Paris) and in the *Landscape* (Mattioli Collection) with the arch of stone that plunges into the ash-colored green of the vegetation. This painting is close in structure to the work of Braque in *The Viaduct of L'Estaque* and one of Picasso's *Landscapes* in the National Gallery, Prague. This new direction includes the thick hedgerow of the 1914 *Landscape* (Jesi Collection) and the *Still Life* (Sheiwiller Collection), which raise the question of how Morandi fits in with the Futurists. Morandi shared Soffici's distrust for Marinetti's movement until 1914. A woman's head drawn in pencil with the date 19 June 1912 carries the imprint of the portraits of Picasso, Cézanne, and also Derain, in whom Apollinaire had recognized "la noble discipline qui purifie la réalité," and the "calme terrible avec lequel il s'exprime sans passion conformément à ses passions." Two surviving versions of *Bathers* and a *Nude* of that year show that Morandi was passing through a phase of orthodox Cubism and Neo-Gothicism. Meanwhile he was most certainly informed of the activities of the Futurists, who were habitually instigating rebellion and anarchy, exalting dynamism rather acritically, and vaunting their intensely "vitalistic" vision. Morandi interpreted the excitement in his own way, adhering to a characteristically cautious perspective of renewal. Most likely he felt no common ground with the many manifestoes that the Futurists published, but he was present at one of the Futurist evening galas that took place amidst quite an uproar at the Teatro del Corso in Bologna on 19 January 1914. Morandi went on to participate in the Esposizione Libera Futurista held in Rome in the same year, though his presence there was marginal. Between 1914 and 1915 Morandi's canvases became denser, with the objects almost huddled together, in stark contrast with the carefully measured pauses that were to become a hallmark of his later work. When the First World War broke out, Morandi was called to arms, and assigned to the Grenadiers. But he fell ill and was declared unfit for military service. When he took up painting once again, there was not a sign in his work of the tragedy that was taking place around him, except perhaps in the ominous ring of objects in the engraving of 1915, in which "it is as if [Morandi] wishes to conjure up the long rifles of the barracks," as Arcangeli put it. All in all, perhaps Morandi's intention was quite simply to survive, and to do so he assumed a detachment from his environment which was to become an essential feature of his work, forging a form of expression that shunned the events of the unfolding history of his day. In the landscapes painted in 1916 the color spreads out in agile tones of green, lilac, and bleached-out earth, and the Cézannian mold serves as a base in which (as with Braque and Matisse) the first hints of Cubism surface in a beguiling interplay of chromatic features. In these works Brandi detected "the echo of pre-Cubist Picasso and the first signs of integrating our Quattrocento." The allusion to Rousseau in the 1916 *Flowers* is clear, and there is a sweet Platonism in the *Still Lifes* with their exhausted tonalities that convey a wholly unexpected virginity of touch. The next year was not an easy one, and the painter's output was sparse. The Mattioli Collection *Cactus* marks the start of a series of works which have been labelled metaphysical, and which are starkly contrasted by the painting *Flowers* from the Vitali Collection.

In 1918 the Rome newspaper *Il Tempo* published the first in-depth article on Morandi, written by the artist's author friend Riccardo Bacchelli. This was followed almost immediately by an article in the Bolognese magazine *La Raccolta* (owned by Giuseppe Raimondi, and to which Carrà also contributed), accompanied by a reproduction of the 1915 engraving. For some time Raimondi acted as a go-between for Morandi and the two leading figures of Italian metaphysical painting, Giorgio de Chirico and Carlo Carrà, as the Bolognese artist did not actually meet them until later. Where the work of Morandi was a crystallization of an elementary fidelity in which all the non-formal functional values of the objects are completely annulled, the objects in the paintings of de Chirico and Carrà communicate their true value as objects, their meaning is dilated and they are given order — the Mediterranean outlook of Carrà is given new structure, and the Nordic imprint of de Chirico is imbued with new meaning. The metaphysical objects of Morandi resided on a more evolved plane of harmony. Their presence, or absence (it no longer mattered) was to become increasingly abstracted in time, and they came to exist in a mental, spatial and temporal dimension. Morandi not only distanced himself from his objects, but made them autonomous to the point of severing them from their symbolic function, until they were totems of a poetic truth that referred to itself alone.

His work had become a process of capturing the truth. The interpenetration of object, light and space is compellingly innovative and becomes total in the metaphysical paintings executed between 1918 and 1919, and any possible symbolization of one element in another is eliminated. Likewise all functional values and communication with the outside world are removed. If we accept that it is intellectual analysis that needs symbols, and that metaphysics can do without them because it refers directly to specific external things, then Morandi is in every sense a metaphysical artist. The poetics of pure art had begun to attract the attention of the finest minds in Europe during this particular period of history, and Morandi was a totally convincing interpreter of the widespread inspiration to achieve the absolute. It is no surprise that the term "purism" was used in reference to Morandi's work, though the equation with Ozenfant and Jeanneret seems somewhat misapplied, as it relegates Morandi's metaphysics to a form of intellectual pastime.

But not even Morandi was able to bear his rarefied atmospheres for long. In the *Still Life* (in the Hermitage Museum) the scene is enlivened with unprecedented flashes of absurdity reminiscent of de Chirico. The still lifes with their magic boxes begin to palpitate with signs of life. The closing gesture of Morandi's metaphysical period, the 1919 *Still Life*, reverberates with the breath and warmth of the commonplace things of everyday life.

The second half of the year marks the retrieval of objective solidity, "things" become opaque with moods, taking on body and seriousness. This signalled a complete departure from the lucidity and unyielding metaphysical rationale pursued earlier, and it emerges most strikingly in the still lifes painted at the close of 1919, which give way to the more domestic forms common to *Valori Plastici*, a magazine which served as an outlet for airing the complex transition from avant-garde expression to one of order. Morandi took heed of the ideas of the day, and shared them briefly. After all, his friend Raimondi had been an active go-between for Morandi and the luminaries, and he had also been the first to attribute an "Italian and traditional" meaning to the concept of "metaphysical" as a countermeasure to the tide of imported Nordic doctrines and rampant Germanism. Then there was Carrà, who even as early as 1920 was seen as a mouthpiece for idealism and artistic nationalism. And his dear friend Soffici was well into his restoration drive.

Between 1919 and 1920 Morandi seemed to gain new insights. At the time, the figures who entertained the most active dialogue with Europe during this return to order in Italian art were, to my mind, Giorgio de Chirico and his brother Savinio, while Morandi modestly opened himself to the ideas that foreshadowed the Novecento. The splendid and inimitable large *Still Life with Pitcher* painted in 1920 signals the transition from Morandi's purely metaphysical stage to that of the *Valori Plastici*, and basically a shift to a more restful, day-to-day tone. The relapse of certain archaisms is fairly evident, and runs parallel to the research Carrà was busy undertaking, but here in this still life we can see the new phase in its most absolute form. The warm terracotta seems to breathe Mediterranean memories, and the shadow is playful. The bottle, the vase, the ball and the fruit-basket are carefully scored in ultra-fine strokes of light and space. The wood of the table also has this warmth and emits a luminous glow like matured honey, rising from within the composition and fixing it in an unreal dimension. No more harsh borders, nor patterns of proud and tense spaces; it is as if a slight breath of wind had disturbed the whole scene. The tone of the painting achieves new depths, and the white settles gently over the shimmering shadow of the vase on the left of the painting, like dried lime on an overturned bottle.

At this point Morandi dispensed with any further experimentation on a linguistic level, and committed himself to a solitary course which he kept to even when he found himself alongside his early traveling companions in group exhibitions. From here on, it was no longer a question of poetics for Morandi, but one of poetry. The outcome was the chaste rashness of his still lifes of 1920, and the retiring flowerpieces with their quiet plasticity, the product of the unflagging exercises he had gone through in his metaphysical period.

In the 1921 still lifes, however, something has shifted once more, especially in the atypical painting from the Morandi Collection with its austere and dramatic undertones. Something in this series would seem to justify Arcangeli's claim that they presage the work of Jean Fautrier, Ennio Morlotti, and of informal naturalism. The almost resentful clustering of the subject matter is a far cry from the serene rhythms that animate the paintings of Corot and Chardin, who were later to ally themselves with the simple and "sublime" Morandi. Perhaps prompted by the sunken, shadowy beauty he had achieved in a small *Jug* etching in 1920, Morandi once again took to etching the following year, and his output is clearly inspired by that master of light and shadow Rembrandt, whose motifs also appear in the *Still Life with Vase, Shells, and Guitar*, and in the small plate entitled *Still Life with Sugar Bowl, Lemon, and Bread*, though in more humble doses. Meanwhile in the *Tennis Court in the Margherita Gardens in Bologna* and other etchings of the same period there are traces of the *Valori Plastici* group, but the rendering is drained, with a Novecento slant, as can be observed in the *Landscape of Chiesanuova* dating from 1924. According to Vitali, signs of a mounting inner crisis can be discerned in the works dating from the early 1920s. It is as if the artist were hesitating at a fork in the road ahead of him. Perhaps these works also betray the turmoil of someone whose points of reference are suddenly threatened. It did not affect all his work however, as very often in the engravings and landscape paintings there is a commanding sense of harmony and poetry. The first warnings of approaching anguish are visible in the paintings focused on the more authentic objects of Morandi's world, his possessions, the things he saw each day, and which never fell out of use. Morandi clung to these humble objects, the last uncontaminated objects in a world he knew only too well was gradually disintegrating around him — the piece of bread, the old clock, the bottle, the almost timid bunch of flowers, or the small courtyard welcoming the passing of friendly footsteps. The house in the 1921 *Landscape* also seems to dwell outside the flow of time, matted with earth and wild overgrowth, desperately void of any human presence — who could possibly inhabit that windowless wall and that clump of trees, so shut in and defensive? As a defense against the disorder of human existence and of the history that was unfolding in the streets and public squares all over the country, Morandi invested in the reality of memory and an "eternal" inner order. This comes across unmistakably in the landscapes painted in Grizzana during the Second World War.

Morandi had found his solace in the poetry of extremes, in the kind of seclusion that exists only as a result of dire illusion. And what better refuge in which to couch illusions, if not the sphere of poetry?

It has been justifiably pointed out that the works Morandi completed between 1919 and 1920 show great variety as a group, more so than the paintings he carried out from the early 1920s on. The work he executed in the years that followed shows considerable alterations of approach, as Morandi was always alert to discussion on form. But all changes took place within the bounds of his own peculiar autarchy. Morandi withdrew from the prevalent Fascism, modeling his life and work on personalities that he considered to represent a human ideal, and on pre-industrial craftsmanship. Morandi's disavowal of the present was made possible by an alternative present that prevented him from being overcome by acute anguish. This alternative was poetry, and Morandi expressed it in his unwavering choice of subject matter, chosen for its outward form. Hence we have those timeless, suspended still lifes and landscapes, presented with absolute consistency. This partly explains why, after the *Self-Portrait* of 1924 and a series of engravings dominated by female faces, Morandi ceased to portray human figures towards the end of the 1930s. Because of this self-willed isolation from the present, Morandi was obliged to uphold an imaginary esthetic ideal, which bore no relation to the social reality around him. His task was to bestow truthfulness and likeness, even on a physical level. Perhaps landscapes and still lifes can be depicted outside the flow of time without losing their truthfulness, but the artist must associate with people, if his portraits are to maintain their likeness. The old outlines of wood, boxes, bottles, wilted flowers, objects of petit-bourgeois existence can uphold their physical truthfulness in the darkness of an attic, or in the private routine of the studio. But the human figure, the faces of those who live alongside us, cannot be sprinkled with the same timeless dust — neither can one abstract them, as they would lose their credibility. Morandi sensed that in order to defend truth from illusion, poetics had to represent a truth that was also probable.

In the 1920 *Landscape* mentioned above with its windowless wall, and in the anxious still lifes of flowers, fruit, and other objects painted between that year and 1924, there is a distinct undercurrent of subdued but noble Ottocento, which likewise filters through into the self-portraits. The 1924 *Self-Portrait* is a good example — there is nothing solemn to be found in the almost opaque face of a thirty-year-old who has grown up in self-imposed solitude. If it were not for the vein of Post-Impressionism discernible in the elegant use of blues, pinks, and grays, we might even speak in terms of hushed realism, of a manner reminiscent of the style fostered in the Romagna region during Papal dominion. Here Morandi reveals his choice, and broaches the grand tradition of pictorial humility. His mentors at this juncture were Corot and Chardin.

In his presentation at the Fiorentina Primaverile exhibition in 1922, Giorgio de Chirico wrote of Morandi that "he observes with the eye of a believer, and the intimate skeleton of these things which are dead to us because of their immobility, are revealed to him in their most consoling aspect, in their eternity." Sometimes this ethereal quality of Morandi's takes on a solid form, or it reappears, mysterious and inaccessible, in an elusive play of subtle light and shade. Here and there the eye can browse more serenely and pick out a set of soft musical motets in the impressions of the *Cornet of Wild Flowers*, the *Striped Vase with Flowers* and the *Courtyard of Via Fondazza*, which, together with the *Landscape of Chiesanuova* represent Morandi's watercolors of 1924. The last of these repeats the motif used in the oil painting of the same title, in which there is a prevailing sense of drained solitude. One can almost hear the footfall of someone imprisoned.

In the engravings *Landscape over the Poggio*, *Landscape with Tall Poplar*, *Still Life with Pears and Grapes* of 1927, and the *Plains of Bologna*, *Haystack at Grizzana*, and *Flowers in a Cornet* set in an oval background, the previous gloom is dissolved in the light of oncoming spring. The same applies for the 1929 *Still Life* oil painting with the fruit-basket and white bottle, and even in the Vitali Collection *Still Life* of 1929/30 in which the objects surge out of the restrained vanity of the browns, pinkish whites, and muted yellow of the bottle, Morandi adroitly conveys a kind of "antique modernity." Born in the crucible of the emotional work of Chardin in the 1700s and elevated to full legitimacy in the high poetics of the paintings of Jean Siméon, the humble poetic object emerges in a kind of "nostalgia of self" in the works of Morandi.

In the *Still Life* of 1929/30 there is a sort of pathetic warning of the process of demolition that would surface with Mario Mafai, and a pauperizing of objects to mere shadows of themselves. "It is as if the object became its own shadow, and the shadow provided the relationship of light and shade to the objects," wrote Brandi on Morandi's output in this period. For nearly a decade, until 1937, both landscapes and still lifes were wrapt in a poignant tension that impregnates the canvas with traces of a merciless erosion. Morandi never become an Impressionist however, except perhaps in that tenuous way common to the "scuola romana" [Roman school] with which he felt a particular affinity.

Expressions of this are unmistakable in the 1935 *Landscape* (now in the Museo Civico d'Arte Contemporanea in Milan), and to an even greater degree in the 1936 *Still Life* (in the Galleria d'Arte Moderna in Bologna). The latter work is perhaps unfinished and signals a kind of threshold in which Morandi's inquiry seems to come adrift and the objects cling to it as survivor shadows. There seems to be a kind of leprosy developing within that threatens to erode the classical order of things. But Morandi was not like Chaim Soutine who looked on at the suicide of forms.

The etchings close the extensive cycle of engravings Morandi embarked on in 1927, and include the 1930 *Still Life*, the 1931 *Still Life with Cloth*, the *Still Life with White Objects on Dark Background*, and the *Group of Zinnias* also from 1931, the *Zinnias in a Vase, View of the Montagnola in Bologna, Grizzana Landscape* all of 1932, *Still Life* and *Still Life in Fine Lines* both of 1933, and the *Large Dark Still Life* of 1934 — all reflecting his vacillation between serenity and nervous tension. The sense of petrification that weighs on the soot-laden tones of the *Large Dark Still Life* reminds one of the funereal silence after an awesome storm. The void evoked by the absences confers an almost inhuman quality to this frozen cluster of "characters," a symbol representing something that never was, nor ever could be. Not since his metaphysical period had Morandi achieved such awesomely complete silences. Nonetheless, he was unable to withstand such tension for long, and his own good sense shepherded him back to more everyday climes, to the "neither happy nor sad" beauty of the limy hills of the Apennines and the opaque affairs of the Bolognese world. Down in Rome, Antonietta Raphael and Mafai had successfully drawn the exhausted and doleful sense of Jewish sentimentalism from their friends in Paris — Chagall, Pascin, Kisling, and Soutine. From 1921 to 1937 Morandi was closer to them than to any other Italian. When they are not encased in a hushed absence, Morandi's aching reflections do not reach the extremes of form. The guarded "expressionism" of Morandi (and I realize full well that I am stretching the meaning of the word) is without doubt one of the finest possible expressions in response to the anguished questions of Europe in the 1930s. But this does not exactly explain Arcangeli's claim to a chain linking Morandi, Soutine, and Scipione on one side, and Fautrier, Dubuffet, Morlotti, and Burri on the other. There is indeed some affinity between some of Fautrier's or Wols' watercolors and those of Morandi, but the conception of poetics is quite different. What remains is Morandi's refined and noble autarchy, even when he is at the peak of his formal dissonance. His subsequent retreat into the perfect harmony of form gave us the classical and serene Morandi on which his legend is founded.

The *Still Life* of 1941 (Mazzotta Collection) with its suspended spatial sense and the tones of color is emblematic of this restored balance, hovering as always between serene vision and unsettled pathos, as can be seen in the Salvaterra Collection *Landscape* and the *Flowers* completed in 1942. The apparent disorder is a kind of declaration of a newly acquired liberty, rather than the explicit mark of past dramas.

Morandi's long friendship with Roberto Longhi, which became even closer in the second half of the 1930s, probably had a great deal to do with this retrieval of formal confidence. Longhi, a scholar on Piero della Francesca, was to declare to an astonished public that Giorgio Morandi was the finest living painter in Italy. As the storm clouds of war began to thicken over Europe (it was the same year in which Picasso's blood-stained *Guernica* was put on exhibition in the Spanish pavilion at the Paris Exposition) Morandi once more reacted by drawing back from the world, just as he had done during the last world conflict. This was the Bolognese artist's personal answer to the burning of Europe — with his aloof and secluded peace. The 1934 *Landscape* from the Vitali Collection is a good example of a canvas that embodies some of Morandi's long-standing loves — Cézanne and Corot, Piero della Francesca and Vermeer, Chardin and Seurat. As in the landscapes of white inaccessible Apennine roads, the 1943 *Still Life* and the *Still Life* of the following year (now in the Centre Pompidou) also communicate the distance Morandi had taken from his surrounding situation, and his rejection of the madness of war. Once again he was removing himself from the relentless currents of time. The war ended, and Morandi's friend Longhi remembers watching him "slowly and sadly pick his way up the bombed-out street" that led out of Grizzana. Against his will Morandi found himself in conflict with the young Neo-Realists, and also with those of the opposite camp who were engrossed in the search for pure formalism. Rallying to his support were Cesare Gnudi, Gian Carlo Cavalli, Carlo Ludovico Ragghianti and Roberto Longhi himself, who had all taken part in the anti-Fascist resistance movement and realized that Morandi's highly particular resistance as a painter was no less meaningful than other means of opposing a dictatorial regime that had attempted to impose a rhetoric of its own. There were others with him as well — the young Arcangeli, Lamberto Vitali, Pallucchini, to name but a few.

Some of Morandi's finest engravings belong to this period — the *Large Still Life with Bottle and Three Objects* executed in 1946 and the *Still Life with Seven Objects in a Tondo* of the previous year. Other important works include the *Still Life with Nine Objects* of 1954 and the *Still Life with Five Objects* of 1956. The small *Still Life with Three Objects* of 1961 completes the cycle, and ties in directly with the paintings of the same period. The 1946 *Still Life* (Vitali Collection) and the 1948 *Still Life* (Morandi Collection) together with the 1949 *Still Life* in the Galleria d'Arte Moderna in Bologna and with the *Flowers* painted in 1950 represent the style Morandi made his own in the post-war years. Everything is expressed in terms of mental order, and one might tentatively describe it almost as a Puristic period. The odorless *Flowers* (Mattioli Collection) also give a hint of the new goal Morandi had set for himself, as do the *Still Lifes* of 1951, 1952, and 1955 of the same collection. From then on, the motifs of his pictures remained unchanged, and his research into the very limits of his art caused him to perform some astonishing feats of poetic transfiguration, a feature that is repeated in the watercolors. The square grouping of figures in a series of still lifes dating from 1953 onwards prompted Rodolfo Pallucchini to draw a direct parallel to the abstractions of Mondrian. But a close look at the *Still Life* of 1956 in the Galleria d'Arte Moderna in Bologna and at the others in the Domeniconi, Fabbri, Mattioli, and Vitali Collections confirms that Morandi's research throughout the 1950s can only really be defined in terms of an approach of ever increasing detachment.

The lightness of expression in the 1961 *Still Life* (Trombadori Collection) and its peculiar spectral arrangement of the objects in patches of light (an effect that also turns up in the watercolors), underscores another dimension of this acutely human "detachment." In the very last landscape and still life paintings, including the *Landscapes* of 1962 and 1963 in the Galleria d'Arte Moderna in Bologna, and the *Still Life* in the Morandi Collection, we can feel the artist retreating from the world, and a bitter cast seems to descend on the sickening greenery of Grizzana and over the luminous ochres that describe the passing away of flowers and objects. The shadows of the houses at the foot of the hillside are inhabited by ghostly presences, and in the drawings, the faltering lines seem to seek out an emptiness in things. The faintest strokes hint at landscapes that quickly dissolve, at objects that are so fragile they crumble under the weight of the slightest shadow. One can sense that for Morandi, painting had become a land of the infinite, a time with no present.

Giorgio Morandi - A Secret World

Lamberto Vitali

Now that Giorgio Morandi has disappeared from our sight, now that we can no longer glimpse that stooped gait of his as he ambled along the ancient porticoes of Bologna, perennially dressed in his gray flannel suit, Morandi is finally re-emerging as "tel qu'en lui-même l'éternité le change." The true Morandi is finally coming to light, the persona of an artist who made no attempt to conceal either himself or his conception of life, his most secret and intimate world — of a man who, even in his most cordial relations with others, was always ready to defend his personal vision, keep his distance, and live his self-imposed isolation.

It is no secret that for many years Morandi's fame extended no further than a very close circle of artist friends, and that he did nothing whatsoever to break free of this "quarantine." Except on a few rare occasions, Morandi actually turned down offers to exhibit his paintings and watercolors, though not out of any fear of criticism, as he was always fully aware of the import of his personal contribution. Outside his own country as well, Morandi had a certain following of people — unassuming, like himself perhaps, but ever attentive. However, recognition has always been modest — even once Morandi had finally received some attention at home, the response of the critics and the public to the first attempts to put together an organic exhibition of the artist's works was certainly unenthusiastic.

And yet, looking back over the early growth and maturation of Morandi's art, we can see now that the prevailing cultural climate of his day held him in exile until the end. Not one of the movements of this century included him — certainly not the Futurists, although Morandi exhibited alongside the leading exponents of that movement — nor the "Strapaese" or town and countryside movement, though the artists of this group were the first to make public the works of Morandi. Likewise Morandi's so-called metaphysical period bears no relation to the equivalent spirit in Carlo

Carrà or even in Giorgio de Chirico; although there are definite traces of influence from that quarter, as a sphere or as a genus of pictorial expression, Morandi's metaphysics is quite alien (and in fact while other artists from Ferrara dubbed their creations with all manner of bizarre and ironic titles, Morandi continued to call his works "still lifes" in the most generic sense throughout this period). Morandi was something of a *parent pauvre* in the *Valori Plastici* group; he was admitted almost out of kindness, and while his work was featured in the magazine, there seemed to be little awareness of the implications of his contribution.

It has become practice among critics and historians alike to outline everything that Morandi was *not*, with the result that both he and his work appear to have been permanently out of step throughout the fifty years of his activity. The truth is that Morandi gives this impression because as an artist he never drew on ephemera, fashions, and affected mannerisms, nor did he cede to political opportunism. Morandi's single-mindedness stemmed from an exacting personal outlook, which affirmed itself right from the outset.

Morandi's early education was a vital source of strength that served him all his life, and this is a point that cannot be stressed enough, since a poor start inevitably marks all that is to follow. Indeed, it was Morandi's youthful start that established the direction of his career — while artists of the previous generation (Umberto Boccioni, Gino Severini, Carrà and others) were drawn to Divisionism in the wake of Giacomo Balla and Gaetano Previati, or became inextricably implicated in Viennese Secessionism, or, worse still, fell under Munich's influence, the twenty-year-old Morandi, a "petit bourgeois" citizen of a suffocatingly provincial Bologna, pushed off in a totally different direction and, in so doing, revealed an almost prescient understanding of his future, the product of a precocious self-awareness.

The admirable and singular balance of artistic sensibility and reason that came so naturally to Morandi was to lead him to intuit Cézanne's vision even from the few black and white reproductions available to him. And it is the French master's approach to composition that emerges in Morandi's earliest canvases. Similarly it was Morandi's exceptional comprehension of tonal values that formed the basis of his art, and explains his taste for Vermeer, Chardin, and Corot (in his Italian period). The search for visual balance in painting was the only approach suited to Morandi's "poetic" world, to that cloistered disposition which showed no interest in anything transitory and random or in treating subjects taken from mundane affairs. For whole decades Morandi's work was characterized by an almost obsessive return to a handful of commonplace objects, like some persistent refrain.

It was in Morandi's nature to study his motifs at some length, to familiarize himself with them as much as possible before translating them to the canvas or the etching plate. This also explains his repeated use of a small number of outdoor scenes for his landscapes, his constant revision of the Apennine hillsides at Grizzana, where he spent many a memorable season working, and found a source of spare, solemn, simplicity in the subject matter that suited his particular composition of masses, and a matching austerity in the tonal relations of the earth and greenery.

Despite the unchanging themes, there was no monotony of effect. Where another artist might have lapsed into sterile repetition, right from the beginning Morandi's pictorial idiom continued to evolve with a variation of solutions that could not have been richer. If we backtrack to the early still lifes Morandi painted in his youth (particularly those of 1916, in which the pinks, silvery grays, and light blues deposited with transparent candor have a lightness that contrasts strongly with the arrangement of the forms) to his very last canvases, it is not hard to see the complexity of Morandi's output; it was the product of constant and painstaking research, which can easily elude the hurried observer, and was rooted in a technique that left nothing to chance or improvisation.

For this very reason, while Morandi started out with the solid background of a classical artist, he never succumbed to nostalgia for other cultures. He revered Giotto and the masters of the early Quattrocento, and this devotion came to the surface in the paintings from his metaphysical period between 1918 and 1920, during which his objects were scored with the restrained passion of intellectual deliberation. The geometric rhythm of his compositions was well matched by an austere palette limited to whites, yellows, earthy browns, and harsh blacks. Morandi's training in the canons of the early Renaissance perfectly addressed his need for an unashamedly puristic form of order, but he did not cast aside a personal world that had already assumed a distinct physiognomy of its own. Everything he went on to do after this metaphysical stage confirms this fact. The solid outlines and borders disappear, the severe light becomes more caressing, and the pattern of the tonal effects embraces the elements of the composition. The softer accents alternate with the more tragic accounts of the shadowy still lifes, whose composition tends to become denser and tighter, locked in a framework that has been meditated upon at great length. Then abruptly there is an increase in the use of dense earthy colors, applied in thick strokes. Finally — and one of the most fascinating developments in Morandi's art — the forms themselves slowly shed the solemn consistency that characterized them throughout the earlier works, and the artist recedes further and further from a textual rendering of his objects until he reaches a fantasy world, no longer inhabited by objects but by ghosts of objects, whose volumes disintegrate before our eyes.

This outline of the metamorphosis of Morandi's art gives an idea of the complexity of the questions the artist put to himself concerning composition, tone, light, color, and form. The solution to these questions was not only to be found by working on canvas, and in fact, Morandi's graphic works developed hand-in-hand with his painting.

It would be futile and inappropriate to attempt to evaluate whether Morandi's expression was more successful in his painting or in his graphic works. Both his painting and graphic art were formulated on the same values; however the two techniques differed in substance, Morandi accorded them equal importance. His etchings stand apart as they have none of the characteristics normally associated with the work of painter-engravers; the etchings amount to a sizeable portion of Morandi's work (a total of one hundred and thirty-three plates), and have no resemblance to his cursive pencil sketches on paper, which were executed with a quick, improvised hand. For Morandi, the technique of etching represented an outlet for something that could be expressed no other way — it was something highly meditated and deliberate that never depended on the chance results that often occur during the etching process. He worked with great skill in an unhurried fashion, aided by the methodical care of a craftsman, as all those who studied under him at the Accademia knew full well. His etchings were therefore not composed of casual strokes, but of precise groups of fine straight lines (especially in those he did later on in life). These were never mechanically executed, but sensitively rendered; clear batches of easily distinguished lines were graded to give different tonal areas. Here as elsewhere, the problem of shading and tone remained central to Morandi's art. In this way his graphic works and his painting moved in a parallel manner, exploring similar ground.

It is a rare event when the last works of an artist show no sign of weakening, or of lame repetition; there are few indeed who succeed in constantly renewing their art. Morandi forged his art anew to the last, without once regressing. After the years out at Grizzana during the Second World War — a memorable interlude that gave us some of the very finest landscape paintings, imbued with both a serene contemplation of nature and a fine veil of melancholy — his return to Bologna brought with it new demands. The composition of the still lifes takes on a compacted, enclosed look with an almost rigid symmetry that frequently emerges as a series of rectangles aligned one against the other. Morandi continued to base his work on the physical reality before him, constantly re-elaborating on it to achieve something increasingly abstract; to some extent this was like a return to the geometric order of his metaphysical period. Once again, Morandi's figurative skill was more than ever the key inspiration of his art, but his vocabulary had altered. At this point his painting tended towards paler colors — a range of whites (with occasional variations), pinks, violets, diaphanous blues, on which he grafted an occasional note of contrast, vibrant and tense.

All this finds both contrast and reconciliation in the forceful precision of composition, which offers almost tangible evidence of the two constant features of all Morandi's work — in certain moments it seems to belong to a profound, twilight mood, while in others it seems quite the opposite. At once gentle and severe, Morandi's art is firmly anchored in the portrayal of reality, but transcends it completely. It is misleadingly simple, so much so that the thematic material seems almost obvious, when in fact it is profoundly complex.

Paintings

1. *Landscape,* 1911.

2. *Portrait of Woman*, n.d. (1912).

3. *Nude*, 1914.

4. *Still Life*, 1914.

5. *Landscape*, 1914.

6. *Still Life*, 1915.

7. *Flowers*, 1916.

8. *Still Life*, 1916.

9. *Still Life*, 1919.

10. *Still Life*, 1918.

11. *Still Life*, 1919.

12. *Flowers*, 1920.

13. *Still Life*, 1920.

14. *Still Life*, 1920.

15. *Flowers*, 1924.

16. *Flowers*, 1924.

17. *Self-Portrait*, 1924.

18. *Garden of Via Fondazza*, 1924.

19. *Still Life*, 1929.

20. *Still Life*, n.d. (1929).

21. *Still Life*, 1929.

22. *Still Life*, 1929-30.

23. *Still Life*, 1936.

24. *Landscape*, 1940.

25. *Still Life*, 1941.

26. *Still Life*, 1941.

27. *Flowers*, 1942.

28. *Flowers*, 1942.

29. *Landscape*, 1941.

30. *Landscape*, 1942.

31. *Landscape*, 1943.

32. *Still Life*, 1943.

33. *Flowers*, 1946.

34. *Still Life*, 1946.

35. *Still Life*, 1948.

36. *Flowers*, 1950.

37. *Still Life*, 1949.

38. *Flowers*, 1950.

39. *Flowers*, 1950.

40. *Still Life*, 1951.

41. *Still Life*, 1952.

42. *Still Life*, 1955.

43. *Still Life*, n.d. (1956).

44. *Courtyard of Via Fondazza*, 1954.

45. *Flowers*, 1957.

46. *Still Life*, 1956.

47. *Still Life*, 1956.

48. *Still Life*, 1957.

49. *Still Life*, 1958.

50. *Still Life*, 1959.

51. *Courtyard of Via Fondazza*, 1959.

52. *Still Life*, 1960.

53. *Still Life*, 1960.

54. *Still Life*, 1961.

55. *Landscape*, 1962.

56. *Landscape*, 1963.

57. *Still Life*, 1963.

Watercolors

6 aprile 918

58. *Bather*, 1918.

59. *Landscape,* n.d. (1956).

60. *Landscape (Interior of Via Fondazza)*, n.d. (1956).

61. *Landscape*, 1958.

62. *Still Life*, n.d. (1960).

63. *Landscape*, n.d. (1959).

64. *Still Life*, n.d. (1959).

65. *Still Life*, n.d. (1962).

66. *Still Life*, n.d. (1962).

Drawings

67. *Still Life*, 1921.

68. *Still Life*, 1928.

69. *Bottles*, 1932.

70. *Shells*, 1932.

71. *Landscape*, 1942.

72. *Still Life with Shells*, 1943.

73. *Flowers*, 1946.

74. *Still Life*, 1948.

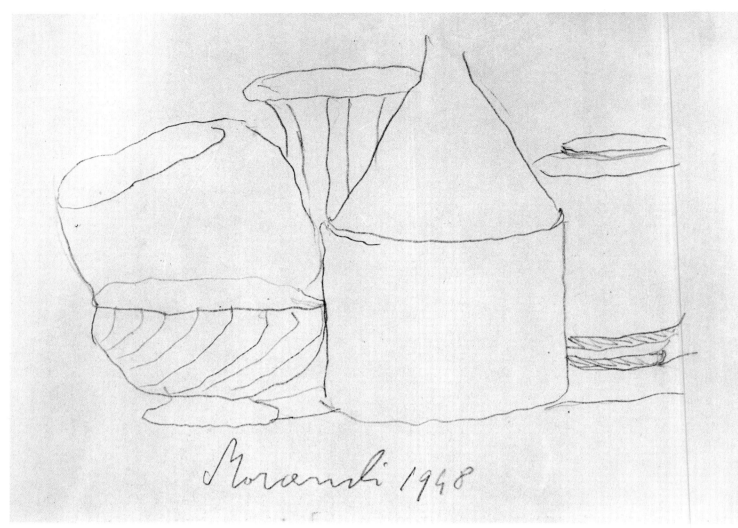

75. *Still Life*, 1948.

76. *Still Life*, 1949.

77. *Still Life*, 1953.

78. *Still Life*, 1958.

79. *Landscape*, n.d. (1960).

80. *Landscape*, 1962.

81. *Flowers*, n.d. (1963).

Etchings

82. *Landscape - Grizzana*, 1913.

83. *Still Life with Vase, Shells and Guitar*, 1921.

84. *Tennis Court in the Margherita Gardens in Bologna* (small plate), 1921.

85. *Still Life with Sugar Bowl, Lemon and Bread*, 1921 or 1922.

86. *Tennis Court in the Margherita Gardens in Bologna* (large plate), 1923.

87. *Landscape of Chiesanuova*, 1924.

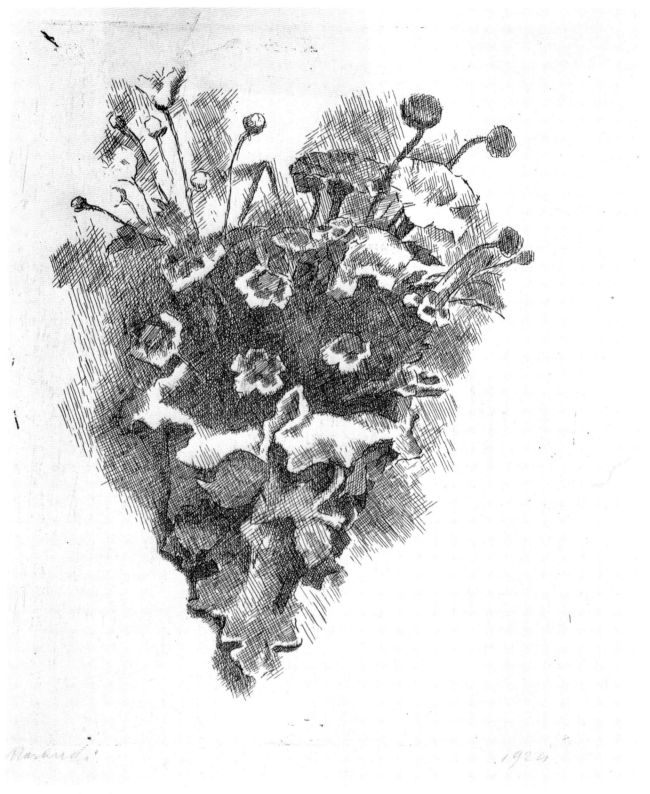

88. *Cornet of Wild Flowers*, 1924.

89. *Striped Vase with Flowers*, 1924.

113

90. *The Garden of Via Fondazza*, 1924.

91. *Landscape over the Poggio*, 1927.

92. *Landscape with Tall Poplar*, 1927.

93. *Still Life with Pears and Grapes,* 1927.

94. *Flowers in a Small White Vase*, 1928.

95. *Landscape (Plain of Bologna)*, 1929.

96. *Haystack at Grizzana*, 1929.

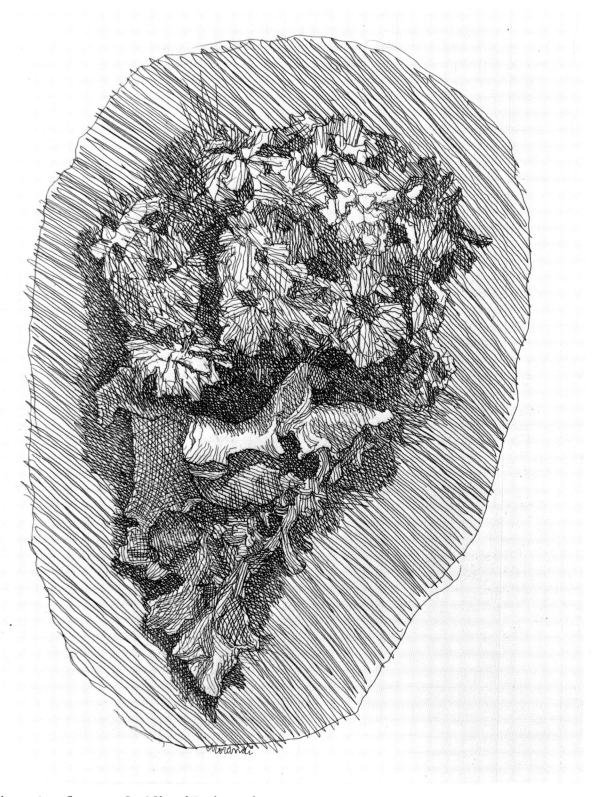

97. *Flowers in a Cornet on Oval-Shaped Background*, 1929.

121

98. *Still Life*, 1930.

99. *Still Life with Cloth*, 1931.

100. *Still Life with White Objects on Dark Background*, 1931.

101. *Group of Zinnias,* 1931.

102. *Zinnias in a Vase*, 1932.

103. *View of the Montagnola in Bologna*, 1932.

Morandi

104. *Landscape of Grizzana*, 1932.

105. *Still Life*, 1933.

106. *Still Life in Fine Lines*, 1933.

107. *Large Dark Still Life*, 1934.

108. *Large Circular Still Life with Bottle and Three Objects*, 1946.

109. *Still Life with Nine Objects*, 1954.

110. *Still Life with Five Objects*, 1956.

Morandi 1961

111. *Small Still Life with Three Objects*, 1961.

112. *Still Life with Seven Objects in a Tondo*, 1945.

Biography

Giorgio Morandi in 1952 (photo by Lamberto Vitali).

With Luigi Magnani in the 1950s.

In his apartment in Via Fondazza in the 1960s (photo by Leo Lionni).

February 1957 (photo by Lamberto Vitali).

In 1961 (photo by Antonio Masotti).

In his atelier in 1960 (photo by Lamberto Vitali).

In the garden in Via Fondazza in 1938 (photo by Francesco Messina).

Biography

Marilena Pasquali

Giorgio Morandi was born in Bologna on 20 July 1890, to Andrea and Maria Maccaferri. He was the eldest of five children, and besides his brother Giuseppe, who died aged eleven, Giorgio had three sisters, Anna, Dina, and Maria, who encouraged and helped him throughout his life.

In 1906 the young Morandi worked in his father's sales office, but, prompted by an artistic disposition, which had manifested itself early, he enrolled at the Accademia di Belle Arti in Bologna. The Morandi family was quick to notice the boy's natural artistic gifts, which are documented in a handful of studies recently brought to the attention of the public by Franco Solmi at the international meeting and exhibition, "Morandi e il suo tempo," held at Bologna's Galleria d'Arte Moderna on 16 and 17 November 1984. The studies include a small painting entitled *Flowers* and two figurines — one of Saint Joseph and one of the Madonna — fashioned in terracotta by the then fifteen-year-old Morandi. These figures found their way into the family Christmas crèche, and are still in the possession of the artist's sisters. Nothing else has survived of Morandi's three-dimensional works, though he must have gone on experimenting for some time after his adolescence. In a well-known article published in 1918, which (as Solmi has pointed out) does not however go into this aspect in great detail, Raffaello Franchi notes that "for Morandi, everything is imbued with the restful atmosphere of the still

life — *even his groups of human figures, which he fashions on clay models* — the perspective marked out in areas of color, each group enclosed and perfect within the contours of its own volume" (R. Franchi, "Giorgio Morandi" in *La Raccolta*, I, nos. 9-10, Bologna, 15 November - 15 December 1918).

On 14 October 1907 the young Morandi enrolled in a preparatory course at the Accademia, and finished it with flying colors. The following October he was promptly admitted to the second year of the foundation course because of his special talents. A few academic drawings from this period (1907-10) are currently in the Accademia di Belle Arti *(Diagram of Pagoda Seen from Side - Layout of Pagoda*, March 1909, and *Corner of a Fifteenth Century House...*, April 1910). Among Morandi's teachers were Domenico Ferri and Augusto Majani, whose comments on his pupil have come to light in a class register from 1909 to 1910. Morandi is recorded as having "feeling for figure," and the grade "6 + " is jotted in the margin of the drawing of 1909. Also studying at the Accademia were Osvaldo Licini and Severo Pozzati, whom Morandi met in 1909.

Morandi's academic record was excellent, and the Accademia duly awarded him a diploma in October 1913. However, during his last two years Morandi ran into conflict with his tutors, ostensibly because of a shift in his interests. He had already begun to tentatively sound out an idiom of

his own, as can be seen in the *Landscape* executed in 1910 (although this still reflects the lingering influence of the Accademia's teaching), in the 1911 *Landscape* from the Vitali Collection, which Cesare Brandi was to describe as "a vast sky of solitude with no respite," and in the *Portrait of the Artist's Sister* dated 1912, in which Giuseppe Raimondi noted a kindred "severity" with the oeuvre of the French painter André Derain during his Gothic period. We should bear in mind that even as early as 1909 Morandi most likely had access to the black-and-white reproductions of Paul Cézanne's works in the volume *Gl'impressionisti francesi*, edited by Vittorio Pica and published the previous year in Bergamo. We can also assume that Morandi followed Ardengo Soffici's series of articles dedicated to *L'impressionismo e la pittura italiana* (which appeared in the journal *La Voce*, I, no 16, 1 April; no 18, 15 April; no 20, 29 April; no 21, 6 May 1909). That year, Morandi visited the Eighth Venice Biennale. And the following year when he returned, Morandi was particularly inspired by the room devoted entirely to thirty-seven works by Auguste Renoir.

In an essay of 1964, Francesco Arcangeli comments that "1910 was the year of Morandi's first two memorable journeys — one to Florence, and one to Venice to see the Biennale. Vitale Bloch relates that 'he still talks of his first trip to Florence — of all the churches where he admired frescoes by Giotto, Paolo Uccello, Masaccio, and of the Uffizi — by evening he was laid up with a shocking fever.' The main purpose of his trip to Venice was to see the Renoirs — many years have passed since I saw Morandi clutching the worn and yellowed reproductions of Renoir's works, torn from the old catalogue.''

In 1911 Morandi went to Rome to visit the international exhibition mounted in celebration of Italy's first fifty years since the Unification, and here he was to see a selection of works by Monet, and Renoir's *Girl with Roses*.

These were crucially formative years for the young artist. In addition to defining and subsequently exploring his chosen sphere of interests and his cultural awareness, Morandi began to infuse his work with characteristics he was to make his own. In 1912 he completed his first etching, entitled *Bridge over the Savena*, produced in a limited edition. Lamberto Vitali has pointed out the "Cézannian mold" and the underlying parallel the etching has with the "singular motif of the gray 1911 *Landscape* which inaugurated his series of paintings."

In the summer of 1913 the Morandi family spent their holidays in the town of Grizzana in the Apennine hillside near Bologna, and here the young Morandi painted his first summer canvases, in which the greenery of Grizzana was to "take root."

Morandi was by no means a solitary person and kept up a keen association with other young artists who, like himself, were alert to anything and everything which would enable them to catalyze an artistic renaissance. Morandi is recorded as being present at the Futurist session in Modena in the spring of 1913, and he also attended the gala evening of Futurism at the Teatro Verdi in Florence on 12 December. In September that year he was given a manuscript by his friend Licini called *I racconti di Bruto*, a series of writings whose form and content were openly provocative. The work, which the author also submitted to Balilla Pratella for publication in the Futurist broadsheet *Lacerba*, refers to a certain "Giorgio" — one of Bruto's comrades in adventure — and "Giacomo" — who is obviously Giacomo Vespignani from nearby Lugo.

By the end of the year Morandi had joined forces with Riccardo and Mario Bacchelli, the sons of Giuseppe Bacchelli, mayor of Bologna and patron of the arts. All three

were to enjoy a lasting friendship with Morandi, and it was through them that the artist met Giuseppe Raimondi.

In January 1914, Morandi visited the exhibition on Futurist "free painting" — Pittura Libera Futurista — set up in Florence by the editors of *Lacerba*. Monopolizing the attention were Umberto Boccioni's *States of Mind*, two of Carlo Carrà's works *The Gallery in Milan* and *Objects in Rhythm*, eighteen works by Ardengo Soffici, and various paintings by Gino Severini and Luigi Russolo. "On 19 January 1914," writes Solmi in an essay published in 1978, "Morandi was at the Teatro del Corso in Bologna for a performance of *Elettricità* by Emilio Marinetti, which took place amidst a frightful uproar. Boccioni, Carrà, Russolo, and Pratella were also present, in solidarity with the author. The encounter clearly bore fruit, as we know that Bacchelli, Licini and Morandi wrote to Boccioni to thank him for sending them some books, and to ask for 'advance news of the next exhibition in Rome' (organized by Sprovieri). Pratella invited us to participate and to notify him of the works we intended to submit, and to send them directly down to Rome. There had obviously been no occasion for Boccioni and Russolo to visit the artists' studios, or they would not have written to Pratella asking him to see personally to choosing the works."

The famous five-man show that took place in the Hotel Baglioni in Bologna on 21 and 22 March was mainly interpreted by the critics as the airing of the Bolognese "secessionists." The public however saw it as an exhibition of "Futurism," an expression they identified with the sheer variety that those years of lively cultural debate had managed to bring to the fore.

As subsequent criticism has accurately pointed out, the fifty works that Morandi, Licini, Mario Bacchelli, Giacomo Vespignani, and Severo Pozzati (at the time a sculptor) exhibited actually represented the first attempt at remolding the spirited but provincial climate of Bologna during the 1910s, though as a group they did not subscribe to any collective or pre-arranged stylistic canons. Morandi submitted thirteen canvases and four pencil drawings; among the paintings were his *Portrait of the Artist's Sister* of 1912, four landscape paintings of 1913 (Vitali, 1977, nos. 6, 7, 8, and 11), two landscapes dating from 1914 (Vita-

li, nos. 16 and 17), and a number of "still lifes with glass," which Ascanio Forti, writing in the Bologna daily *Il Resto del Carlino* on 22 March 1914, defined as an "intermingling of glasswork in twilight." One of these still lifes and a drawing were included in the first Esposizione Libera Futurista a few days later, organized at the Galleria Sprovieri in Rome from 13 April to 25 May. However, the autonomy Morandi managed to maintain, and the distance between his own artistic standpoint and that of the organized Futurist mainstream is evident in the *Snow Landscape* of 1913 which he presented to the Second Secession exhibition in Rome. The program of the show excluded the Futurists, and it was here that Morandi had the chance to witness a whole wall of paintings by Matisse, and a room given over entirely to watercolors by Cézanne.

Despite his fascination with the pursuits of the Futurists, Morandi was quite independent from Marinetti's movement, and his work is noticeably closer on a cultural level to the achievements of the Cubists on the other side of the Alps who were working on the germinal pattern created by Cézanne. This affinity can be seen in the still lifes Morandi completed in 1914 and 1915.

Morandi's academic career began with his appointment as a drawing teacher in elementary schools for the Bologna Council, a post he was to keep until 1929.

In 1915 he was called to military service and assigned to the Second Regiment of Grenadiers stationed at Parma. After six weeks he became critically ill and was admitted to the local army hospital, and later sent home, declared unfit for further military service.

These were years of hard work and meditation in close company with other young Bolognese intellectuals such as Giuseppe Raimondi and Bino Binazzi. However, few works survive from this period; as Lamberto Vitali recalls in his monograph of 1964, Morandi destroyed a great many of them. We have a few versions of *Bathers* of 1915, the 1916 *Landscapes* from the Jesi and Maccari Collections, the *Flowers* from the Vitali Collection, dating from 1917, the two compelling spiral *Still Lifes* of 1916 and the *Still Life* of the same year now at the Museum of Modern Art in New York.

In the winter of 1917 Morandi was once

again seriously ill, and the paintings that survive from this year include a cogently rhythmical summer *Landscape,* a painting with a metaphysical slant entitled *Cactus,* and the *Self-Portrait* published in 1918 in *Valori Plastici* but later destroyed by the artist.

Also dating from 1917 is Morandi's association with the inter-regional exhibition held in Lugo in November. Morandi submitted *Houses in the Snow* and six watercolors with the title *Impressions of the Bologna Foothills.*

This signalled the start of Morandi's deeply metaphysical period. In his celebrated definition of the situation, Cesare Brandi (Florence, 1942) wrote that "a group of key still lifes belongs to the years 1918 and 1919, in which we can notice emerging from the flat formulation a carefully composed exegesis of the volumes, surfacing in the impenetrable wholeness of light blue, pushed to such limits, and so cold, that they lose the usual abstract sense of archetypal forms — the cylinders, cones, and ovoids are merely hinted at and never visualized, inhabiting a purely mental plane."

On 29 March 1918 the young Morandi landed his first monographic review in the Rome daily *Il Tempo,* written by Riccardo Bacchelli. The Bologna journal *La Raccolta* owned by Giuseppe Raimondi promptly followed suit, publishing an excerpt of the monograph in the second issue of the journal (dated 15 April) with an accompanying reproduction of the watercolor *Still Life with Bottle and Jug* (1915), which adopts the same alertly structured and sinuous forms common to the paintings of this period. It was apparently in 1919 that the Bolognese artist first met Giorgio de Chirico, during a trip Morandi made with his friend Raimondi to Rome in the first half of August (letter from Morandi to Raimondi dated 15 August 1919, published in the book *Anni con Giorgio Morandi* by Giuseppe Raimondi, Milan, 1970). That summer, Carrà was passing through Bologna, and on 28 August Morandi invited him to stay in his house at 34 Via Fondazza. Carrà showed a keen interest in the paintings of the Bolognese artist "particularly in the later ones, but also in the earlier ones with their flowers and bottles, which I have hung on the walls" (letter dated 30 August 1919). In September Carrà wrote to Riccardo Bacchelli asking for photographs of Morandi's

works, as he intended to write an article, to be published in a Milanese magazine together with a few reproductions (letter dated 17 September 1919).

During his trip to Rome, Morandi also became acquainted with the literary luminaries of *La Ronda* who had invited Giuseppe Raimondi to the capital. These were Emilio Cecchi, Vincenzo Cardarelli, Antonio Baldini, and the artist of the group, Armando Spadini.

Towards the end of 1918 Raimondi also introduced Morandi to Mario Broglio, who on 15 November had launched the publication *Valori Plastici.* Broglio offered Morandi a contract, the details of which were discussed later in the course of a visit by the Roman artist to Bologna in November (letter dated 17 November 1919), and later finalized on 26 December 1919. Although Morandi had committed himself to working exclusively with the *Valori Plastici* group for eighteen months (and in fact his collaboration was to last until the group broke up), his first works were bought by Broglio and his partners — who included the Roman tailor Martellotti and Mario Girardon — as early as March 1919. According to Vitali, these works were the gray *Landscape* of 1911, the *Landscape* from the Jesi Collection, dated 1913, and the Jucker Collection *Landscape* of the same year. The April-May issue of *Valori Plastici* featured a reproduction of the *Still Life* (Orombelli Collection, 1918) and an *Avvertimento Critico* written by Raffaello Franchi centered on the work in question. Other works by Morandi appeared in the November-December issue of the Rome magazine (two still lifes and a self-portrait), and the cover of the third issue of 1921 featured Morandi's watercolor *Nude.* The fourth issue of the same year, which was illustrated throughout with no less than eleven of the Bolognese artist's works, featured seven oil paintings executed between 1911 and 1920, and four watercolors dating from 1918.

This account clearly illustrates the intensity of the rapport Morandi enjoyed with the more active cultural fronts in Italy, and not only the artistic ones. Morandi kept a lively correspondence with Ottone Rosai (letter to Giuseppe Raimondi dated 4 December 1919), and revived his friendship with Vincenzo Cardarelli who stayed with the Bacchelli family in Bologna from April 1920

through to the summer. Eight years later, Cardarelli would ask Morandi to illustrate a collection of poems entitled *The Sun at Noon* with drawings from the artist's etchings.

In 1920 Morandi resumed his engraving work, which he had set aside five years earlier, with two etchings (*The Environs of Bologna* and *Jug*). He pursued his engraving intensely until mid-way through the 1930s, particularly between 1927 and 1932.

Mario Broglio held fast to his commitment, and organized an exhibition for the group in Berlin for March 1921, with works by Giorgio de Chirico, Carrà, Morandi, Arturo Martini, Roberto Melli, Edita Walterowna von Zur Mühlen, and Ossip Zadkine. Morandi was allocated an entire room to himself with nineteen major paintings, and numerous etchings and watercolors. Among the oil paintings submitted were *Large Still Life with Mannequin, Mannequin with Round Table,* and *Still Life with Skittle.* The exhibition was subsequently taken to Dresden, Hannover, and Munich. At the Fiorentina Primaverile exhibition the following year the group re-formed, welcoming newcomers both young and old, as well as established figures such as Armando Spadini. The show included works by Carlo Carrà, Giorgio de Chirico, and Ugo Giannattasio, with a critical commentary by Mario Broglio, while the works of Arturo Martini, Cipriano Efisio Oppo, Quirino Ruggeri, Armando Spadini, and Edita Broglio were introduced by Alberto Savinio. Accorded the same importance as de Chirico and Carrà, Morandi had a room to himself with nineteen oil paintings, watercolors, and drawings. "He observes with the eye of a believer," wrote de Chirico in his introduction to Morandi's work which was included in the catalogue, "and the intimate skeleton of these objects, whose stillness makes them seem dead to us, is captured by him in its more consoling aspect, *in its eternity.* By so doing, he participates in the great lyricism styled by the latest current of European art, namely *the metaphysics of everyday objects,* of those objects we have become so accustomed to that we tend to observe them with the eye of someone *who looks without being aware of it...*" With respect to the works Morandi executed over these years, we can agree with Lamberto Vitali (1964) when he says that "the large *Still Life with Round Table* (Vitali Collection, 1977, no 51) is a kind of bridge between the artist's so-called metaphysical period and the period immediately following. It loses nothing of the achievements to date, and at the same time it seems to unveil a truer face of Morandi the artist. While the composition is mindfully orchestrated with a perfect awareness of space and interval, the pictorial idiom is a presentiment of all that was to follow, right up to the present day." Together with the *Still Life with Round Table and Pitcher* are various works dating from 1920 that offer a glimpse of the numerous potential paths that branched out before the artist, namely the *Still Life with Glass, Bread and Knife* (now in Düsseldorf), the forcefully plastic *Still Life* in the Galleria d'Arte Moderna in Bologna, and the intense and somber *Still Life* (private collection in Bologna, Vitali, nos. 53, 57, and 59). In Vitali's words "The older masters and Cézanne had served as mentors throughout the first decade; now other simulacra were set alongside these before the altar, artists such as Chardin, and in particular Corot. Previously these guides had been chosen more through intuition than through material knowledge of their works... The series of landscapes from 1921 to 1925 could scarcely have come about without the example of Corot to draw on — not just for the severe tonal execution, but for the cogent paring down of motifs to the essentials, discarding minor features..." (for confirmation see the *Landscape* of 1921 belonging to a private collector, and the *Landscape* of Villa Comi of 1922, and the *Landscape of Chiesanuova* of 1925 in the Jesi Collection). Morandi was by no means absent from the more salient events of cultural debate, and took part in the Novecento Italiano exhibition at the Galleria Permanente in Milan in the February-March session 1926, and later in March and April 1929. At the first session he displayed three works, one *Still Life* which Mussolini purchased for 600 lire, the 1924 *Self-Portrait* held in a private collection in Milan (Vitali, no 96), and the 1925 *Landscape* owned by the Banco di Roma (Vitali, no 108). At the second exhibition, in 1929, he entered three etchings, including two still lifes, two drawings entitled *Head of a Girl* and *Still Life*, and three oil paintings — the *Landscape* of 1927

(Vitali, no 119), a still life dated 1928 (Vitali, no 128), and a second still life. Although he did not take an active part in the group's pursuits, Morandi submitted his works on a number of occasions, including the exhibition set up by Mario Tozzi in the Galerie Bonaparte in Paris in November 1929 (one still life etching), and the shows held in Basel (January and February 1930) and Bern (from March to May). Another key occasion was the exhibition mounted by the group led by Margherita Sarfatti in Buenos Aires and Brazil, once again in 1930. In March 1932 a special exhibition opened in the Galerie Georges Bernheim, Paris, focusing on twenty-two artists representing the "Artistes italiens modernes," who included the major exponents of Italian art of of the inter-war period, namely Felice Casorati, Giorgio de Chirico, Filippo de Pisis, Alberto Savinio, Scipione, and Morandi.

Morandi showed a certain affinity to the intellectual group involved with the journal *Il Selvaggio* which was first published in 1924 under the guidance of Mino Maccari. Morandi joined the group and took part in the second international exhibition of modern engraving held in Florence in 1927. In addition to publishing various works by Morandi in the journal, on 8 June Maccari dedicated a long article to him in the Bologna newspaper *Il Resto del Carlino*, stating that "Morandi's art epitomizes Italian art, and is deeply rooted in the national tradition." This opinion was taken up with added vigor by Leo Longanesi on 31 December 1928 in the newspaper *L'Italiano*. Longanesi called Morandi the "finest example of *Strapaese* we have." The consecration of the "Italian-ness" of Morandi's art came about just four years later in March 1932 when the tenth issue of *L'Italiano* was dedicated to Morandi, with a critical text by Ardengo Soffici, who had since become one of the country's leading critics.

That year Morandi made his debut at the Venice Biennale. At the 1928 session he exhibited four etchings and a folder of engravings in the Sala del Bianco e Nero (*Landscape with the Large Poplar*, 1927, Vitali, 1964, no 34; two other landscapes, and a still life). In 1930 he submitted two etchings to the Sala del Bianco e Nero (*Little Garden* and *Still Life*) and four paintings to Sala 14, which included a 1930 *Self-*

Portrait, Flowers of 1924, and two still lifes dating from 1929 (Vitali, nos. 159, 92, 141, 146). At the Nineteenth Venice Biennale in 1934 Morandi was present once more in the Sala del Bianco e Nero with two still lifes and an etching.

From 1929 onwards, he also exhibited his works frequently outside Italy — in addition to the Novecento Italiano exhibition, Morandi was also invited to submit works for the Carnegie Award in Pittsburgh (and was to return the following year, in 1933, 1936, and three other times after the Second World War). In 1930 Morandi was present at the exhibition of modern engraving set up at the Bibliothèque Nationale in Paris. The following year he sent a still life of 1929 (Vitali, no 143) to the Settimana Italiana exhibition held in Athens. In 1933 Morandi was also present at the Künstlerhaus in Vienna for the exhibition Moderne Italienische Kunst where he presented a still life of 1929 (Vitali, no 141 — the same one he submitted for the 31st Carnegie Award the same year). In 1934 his works appeared at the Mostra d'Arte Italiana organized by the Venice Biennale in North America, and the following year there was a large-scale exhibition of Italian art spanning both 19th and 20th centuries at the Musée du Jeu de Paume in Paris, organized jointly by the Italian and French governments. The French press felt that Morandi was "mal placé," and in fact his two still lifes of 1935 (Vitali, nos. 191, 192) were hung in a corner near a decorative vitrine containing ceramics by Pietro Melandri and Ravasi. In 1936 Morandi's paintings were featured in a show held in the Italian pavilion at the Exposition Universelle in Paris, and later in the following year Morandi was invited to a large exhibition which the Venice Biennale authorities organized in Berlin. He was also invited to the next exhibition staged at the Kunsthalle in Bern (1938), where four of the artist's works were on show. Although he applied for a passport that year, Morandi did not take any further trips abroad, but watched for exhibition opportunities on the international front, and entered the more significant ones. In 1939 Morandi sent a group of particularly notable works to the Golden Gate Exhibition in San Francisco (*Self-Portrait* from the Zoja Collection, a 1914 *Landscape* from the Mattioli Collection, a *Still Life* of 1918 from the Jesi Collection, the dark *Still Life* of 1924 from the Longhi Collection, and the *Landscape* of 1936 from a private collection in Milan, Vitali, no 219). Also in 1939, one of Morandi's etchings belonging to the collection of the Calcografia Nazionale appeared at the special exhibition on etching held at Kaunas in Lithuania under the auspices of the Ministry of Cultural Affairs; and the following year Morandi exhibited his works at the grand exhibition of Italian art in Zurich.

The course of Morandi's academic career is an equally clear indicator of the fame and esteem he enjoyed in intellectual and official circles in his day. After many years of teaching in municipal art schools, in 1929 Morandi moved to the art college as an instructor in figure drawing. Then in 1930, mid-way through the academic year he was appointed directly to the body of permanent teachers at the Accademia di Belle Arti in Bologna, with a Professorship in Intaglio — a position which until then had been held by Augusto Majani (letters dated 8, 9, 25, and 30 April 1930 between the President of the Accademia, Iginio Benvenuto Supino, and the Minister of Public Education, filed in the Accademia archives in Bologna). The artist was to go on teaching until 1 October 1956, when he asked to step down "after 26 years and 8 months" of teaching, during which he had instructed several generations of young artists in the skills of engraving.

In 1931 Morandi participated at the First Quadriennale of national art which opened at the Palazzo delle Esposizioni in January in Rome in Sala 39 where other Bolognese artists including Lea Colliva, Nino Bertocchi, Guglielmo Pizzirani, Gianni Poggeschi, Garzia Fioresi, Gino Marzocchi, and Bruno Saetti were also exhibiting works. Morandi won an award for his contribution, which consisted of three still lifes in oil (Vitali, nos. 147 and 157), a drawing (*Head of a Youth*) and two still life etchings. At the second session of the Quadriennale in 1935 Morandi submitted two landscape paintings and two still lifes (Vitali, nos.174, 164, and 170), as well as two etchings. But it was with the Third Rome Quadriennale that Morandi's position in the art world was confirmed. Certain respected scholars had already spoken out very much in favor of Morandi's art, including Roberto Longhi. In his inaugural lecture for the

academic year 1934/1935 at Bologna University, Longhi gave a critical outline of Bolognese painting "Momenti della pittura bolognese," and ended it with a pointed reference to Morandi, describing him as "one of the finest living painters in Italy." Morandi had an entire exhibition room to himself, with forty-two oils, two drawings, and twelve etchings. He won the second prize for painting, just behind the younger artist Bruno Saetti. Some of the leading critics of the day took his side, including Cesare Brandi and Giuseppe Marchiori; the young Duilio Morosini applauded him in *Corrente*, and Arnaldo Beccaria who, apart from devoting articles to the artist in the Milan magazine, published a monograph on him that year. However, there were also dissenters who accused Morandi of casting a "veil of drabness over his pictures," creating a "dim and gray salon" in which the paintings became "all the same, regulated, adjusted and set in line" — this was Osvaldo Licini writing his impressions in a letter to Marchiori on 3 March. Licini continued to fuel the debate, allying himself with Carlo Belli, who answered Beccaria through the pages of the *Corriere Padano*, a newspaper published in Ferrara. Licini likewise agreed with Luigi Bartolini (for different reasons however) who launched an attack on Morandi (his friend from the late 1920s) through the publication *Quadrivium* criticizing "those modest and sincere compositions of earlier times, painted as studies, which now have an academic slant to the tones and forms, and have become parlor pieces."

In the midst of these polemics over his work, Morandi pressed ahead, encouraged by worthy critics such as Longhi, Brandi, Vitali, Gnudi, and Ragghianti. Work in the studio in Via Fondazza went on without a break, and in the summer Morandi moved to Grizzana, where he painted canvases such as the 1939 *Still Life* (Plaza Collection, Caracas), *Flowers* (Longhi Collection) and *Still Life* (National Gallery, Berlin) both executed in 1940, the Jucker Collection *Still Life* and the *White Road* of 1941, the *Still Life* (Gnudi Collection, bequeathed to the Galleria d'Arte Moderna, Bologna), and the two Magnani Collection *Still Lifes* dated 1943 (the "compositions of objects" such as the one from the Boschi Di Stefano donation to the Galleria Civica, Milan, and the "shells" in which Arcangeli saw hints

of Chaim Soutine.) The *Still Life* of the Brandi Collection is an exceptional example of this group.

World conflict was reaching a climax, and after observing for a few days the fate of his friends from the "Justice and Freedom" group — Longhi, Ragghiani, Gnudi and other intellectuals of the Bolgnese circuit, who were arrested in June 1943 — Morandi withdrew to Grizzana. "This period in Bologna and Grizzana was truly magnificent for Morandi," wrote Arcangeli. "Until the bombing began to really lay waste to the country, it was as if Morandi was protecting us with that aloof and profound horizon of his. Looking back, I'd say the life he lived was rich in experience. Though the nation was at the end of its tether, the first inklings of re-found liberty began to surface from the deep sea of dismay, and there was a burgeoning group of admirers around Morandi. Although he had not yet achieved fame, he was warmly and openly acknowledged. In addition to the first book by Brandi, Raimondi wrote his most glowing accounts during these years — for a few seasons we could not help but admire Morandi, disinterestedly and openly, even revere him... Longhi, Raimondi, Brandi, Ragghianti, Gnudi, the youngest of us (the most passionate admirer of all, Alberto Graziani is no longer alive) were all there. Despite everything, Morandi had never once become estranged from that illusion of freedom — he had channelled it in his highly personal way, vesting it with a human and wholly credible dimension, and who knows how deeply he felt that solitude which he had always reserved for himself — a solitude in which we were all suddenly obliged to make drastic decisions. Morandi's state of mind is eloquently testified to by a handful of paintings. I can remember my one and only visit to Grizzana, in April 1944, when I saw an unfinished landscape now belonging to a private collection in Rome that had already taken on an exquisite form. My excitement was due less to the harmony (which Morandi seemed determined to tease out from the air of incumbent disaster) than to the light within the painting — diaphanous, immersed in a glow of earliest spring, pale and alluring. This was the light of a season which simply had no more need of Man, but which seemed to lean on the dimensions he had created — the earliest and most meagre suggestions of the roofs, the luminous walls, the humble traces of paths, the engaging meadows. Something seemed to refer back to a suspended time of origin or extremity of civilian life, a sort of 'primal state' which opposed nothing, and which for this reason perhaps was all the more frightening. Morandi felt this sense of extremity I am referring to, without confessing it, and transmitted it in some of his paintings..."

In the spring of 1945 Roberto Longhi presented a one-man show of Morandi's at the Galleria Fiore in Florence in homage to his friend. No sooner was the war over than the polemics returned, this time on the issue of commitment in art. A text by Cesare Gnudi based on an idealistic and Crocian standpoint published in Florence in 1946 was a direct answer to Antonello Trombadori who, writing for the publication *Rinascita*, tabled a discussion on "Seriousness and limits in the work of Morandi." The Venice Biennale in 1948 saw the emergence of the "Fronte nuovo delle arti," and it was no surprise that the first prize for painting was awarded to Morandi, who had eleven key canvases dated between 1916 and 1920 on display in the room dedicated to "Three Italian painters from 1910 to 1920." Alongside those of Morandi were works by Carrà and Giorgio de Chirico, with an introduction by Francesco Arcangeli. (The paintings submitted by Morandi were the two *Still Lifes* and *Flowers* of 1916, the metaphysical *Still Lifes* of 1918-19, and the *Still Life with Round Table and Pitcher* of 1920.)

In order to underscore the importance of Morandi's graphic works in relation to his paintings, that same year Carlo Alberto Petrucci organized an anthology of Morandi's etchings at the Calcografia Nazionale in Rome which won a great deal of attention from both press and public.

Morandi found himself welcomed in the most exclusive international circles, and his works were included in prestigious exhibitions in northern Europe and in the United States. As if to consolidate this critical esteem, Morandi was awarded the prize for engraving at the Second Biennale of San Paolo, Brazil, in 1953, and went on to win the first prize for painting at the fourth session. The list of exhibitions held abroad that included works by Morandi gives a clear idea of the great success the artist en-

joyed. He had important one-man shows at the Palais des Beaux-Arts in Brussels in 1949 (graphic works), at the Gemeentemuseum in the Hague, at the New Burlington Galleries in London in 1954, at the Kunstmuseum in Winterthur in 1956, at the World House Gallery in New York in 1957 and 1961, at Siegen in 1962 (where he received the Rubens Prize), and at the Badischer Kunstverein in Karlsruhe in 1964.

Giorgio Morandi died on 18 June 1964 in Bologna, after nearly a year's illness.

The same year the first historical and critical overview of Morandi's artistic personality and work began to take shape, thanks to a number of full-scale studies. The first of these was the fundamental monograph by Lamberto Vitali published by the Galleria Milione in Milan, which for decades had diligently followed the master's activity. The second was Francesco Arcangeli's empassioned account, also published by the Galleria Milione. Flanking these works were various writings by Marco Valsecchi (Garzanti, Milan) and by Alberto Martini (Fabbri, Milan). The full catalogue of Morandi's graphic works, compiled by Vitali in 1957, was also published in 1964 in a revised and corrected third edition.

Two years later, the extensive exhibition set up in October at the Archiginnasio in Bologna by Roberto Longhi, GianAlberto Dell'Acqua, and Lamberto Vitali was linked up with the Venice Biennale of that summer, where an important exhibition dedicated to Morandi's work had been held; this was a prime occasion for both critics and public to assess the long course of his art. The exhibition comprised works dating from 1911 to 1963 (in all one hundred and eight oil paintings, fourteen watercolors, thirty-three drawings, and one hundred and thirty-one etchings). On this occasion, the *Portrait of the Artist's Sister* was put on display for the first time since the legendary exhibition held at the Hotel Baglioni in March 1914.

Despite widespread critical acclaim in the last few years of his life (and throughout the 1960s and 1970s), Morandi remained somewhat isolated and removed from the forum of debate that animated the international art scene (and his work was felt by too many as something moderated, coherent, and official). After the debate be-

tween abstract art and realism, between form and content in the 1950s, and after the dramatic season of Informal art (Arcangeli's well-meaning attempt to slot Morandi into the Po Valley tradition of "last naturalists" was in fact disclaimed by the artist himself), the 1960s saw the beginning of a rejection of the very idea of the "opus," an attitude which led to the proclamation of the "death of art" in the 1970s.

Morandi's oeuvre had come to symbolize a highly refined formal mold and poetic expression, and was seen as a form of teaching against the excesses of the avant-garde. Despite the fact that his work had been known and respected for a long time, it had never itself been the object of discussion. It is only recently, largely due to the major exhibitions held in the last few years as a result of the change in cultural climate, that the inescapable fascination of Morandi's painting has been recognized, and the artist has taken his place definitively alongside the masters of the 20th century.

The exhibitions organized by the Galleria Nazionale d'Arte Moderna in Rome in May 1973, and by the Bologna City Council in 1973 at the Hermitage Museum in Leningrad and at the Pushkin Museum in Moscow (organized by Lamberto Vitali, Irina Antonova, and Franco Solmi) played a large role in increasing the exposure of Morandi's work. Such exhibitions have given the public a greater opportunity to study the artist's work. In May 1975, Solmi included a special anthology on Morandi in the inauguration program for the new Galleria Comunale d'Arte Moderna in Bologna. Once again, the anthology was entrusted to the mindful care of Lamberto Vitali, and Solmi wrote "This exhibition on Giorgio Morandi put together by Lamberto Vitali is an event in itself for the critical depth and sheer scope of the quantity and quality of the works on display. The various events have been organized so as to offer an organic arrangement of the opening activities for the new Galleria d'Arte Moderna in Bologna, and this exhibition on Morandi assumes a meaning that goes far beyond the straightforward though much-needed presentation of a substantial body of Morandi's works to the public and to scholars arriving from all over Europe: it gives us a supreme occasion for fulfilling a fundamental need for a comprehensive exhibition — which is essentially a matter of method — something we firmly believe in, and which we intend to adopt in the future, as far as we possibly can." This was an overture to the argument for the Museo Morandi. At the time, the gallery owned only one painting by Morandi. Through donations from the artist's sisters, Anna, Dina, and Maria Teresa, in the years that followed, the main body of works in oil reached a new total of twelve, accompanied by thirty-one etchings and two drawings. With the donations by Cesare Gnudi and Camilla Malvasia, four more oil paintings were added to the collection.

In 1978, a new full-scale retrospective opened at the Palazzo dei Diamanti in Ferrara, with works dating from 1912 through to 1964, enhanced by the entire Ingrao Collection — twenty-two paintings handpicked by the artist himself for the Roman collector Ingrao, and handed over gradually between 1946 and 1963. Coinciding with the event was Franco Solmi's probing study undertaken from 1966 to 1968, which had remained unpublished because of the cultural dissonance of the times. Later, in 1981 and 1982, a major show was organized in Munich by Franz A. Morat, who in 1984 set up a special foundation in Fribourg with one hundred and twenty works (including twenty-four paintings, ten watercolors, forty-three drawings, and forty-eight etchings), and other key exhibitions in San Francisco, New York, and Des Moines (at the Des Moines Center). In Italy, the Brera and Municipal collections were re-organized and considerable emphasis was given to the works of Morandi. Meanwhile the Fondazione De Fornariis reached completion, enabling the Turin Council to purchase twenty-two of Morandi's works including drawings, watercolors and oil paintings. By unanimous public request, work on the Museo Morandi, which was to be sited within the Galleria d'Arte Moderna in Bologna, was also stepped up. A designated area for Morandi's work has been open since 1982, and there is also a special Archive and Study Center now in operation that benefits from the collaboration of Morandi's sisters and the leading Italian and foreign institutes, set up to collect material on the life of the Bolognese master. In the summer of 1985 the Museo Morandi collection was enhanced by a further twenty-two paintings (previously in the Ingrao Collection in Rome), purchased by the Bologna Council for the Museo Morandi.

On 9 November 1985, the Galleria d'Arte Moderna in Bologna opened its doors on the exhibition, "Morandi e il suo tempo," which placed Morandi's work in the context of that of other leading contemporaries on both the national and the international scenes (the collection included over one hundred paintings dating from 1905 to 1964). Scheduled to coincide with the Bologna event came the exhibition at the Brera Museum in Milan entitled "Morandi — 100 Works on Paper."

The Museo Morandi in Bologna currently has seventy-five works in its possession. On 12 June 1987 a major retrospective exhibition on Morandi with one hundred works including paintings, watercolors, drawings, and etchings, opened at the Hôtel de Ville in Paris.

Select Bibliography

A. Beccaria, *Giorgio Morandi*, Ulrico Hoepli, Milan, 1939.

C. Brandi, *Morandi*, Le Monnier, Florence, 1942; 2nd edition revised and updated, Florence, 1952; reissued in *Scritti sull'arte contemporanea*, Turin, 1976.

G. Scheiwiller, *Giorgio Morandi*, Chiantore, Turin, n.d. (1943).

G. Marchiori, *Giorgio Morandi*, Editrice Ligure Arte e Lettere, Genoa, 1945.

C. Gnudi, *Morandi*, Edizioni U, Florence, 1946.

M. Ramous, *Giorgio Morandi - I disegni*, Cappelli, Bologna, 1949.

F. Arcangeli, *12 opere di Giorgio Morandi*, Edizioni del Milione, Milan, 1950.

A. Nigro, *Giorgio Morandi incisore*, thesis, reporter Rodolfo Pallucchini, Università di Bologna, academic year 1951-1952.

P.M. Bardi, *16 dipinti di Giorgio Morandi*, Edizioni del Milione, Milan, 1957.

L. Vitali, *Giorgio Morandi - Opera grafica*, Einaudi, Turin, 1957; 3rd edition revised and updated, Einaudi, Turin, 1964.

C. Brandi, *Ritratto di Morandi*, All'Insegna del Pesce d'Oro, Milan, 1960.

L. Vitali, *Giorgio Morandi*, Edizioni Olivetti, Ivrea, 1961.

L. Vitali, *Giorgio Morandi pittore*, Edizioni del Milione, Milan, 1964; 3rd edition updated, Milan, 1970.

M. Valsecchi, *Morandi*, Club Internazionale del Libro d'Arte, Garzanti, Milan, 1964.

F. Arcangeli, *Giorgio Morandi*, Edizioni del Milione, Milan, 1964; 2nd edition, Einaudi, Turin, 1981.

A. Martini, *Giorgio Morandi*, "I maestri del colore", Fabbri, Milan, 1964.

J. Siblik, *Giorgio Morandi*, Prague, 1965.

J. Leymarie, *Acquarelli di Morandi*, Edizioni de' Foscherari, Bologna, 1968.

G. Marchiori, *Morandi - Le incisioni*, Ronzon, Rome, 1969.

C. Brandi, *Morandi lungo il cammino*, Rizzoli, Milan, 1970.

G. Raimondi, *Anni con Giorgio Morandi*, Mondadori, Milan, 1970.

J.P. Szucs, *Morandi*, Corvina Kiadò, Budapest, 1974.

V. Zurlini, *Il tempo di Morandi*, Prandi, Reggio Emilia, 1975.

N. Pozza, *Morandi - I disegni*, Franca May, Rome, 1976.

L. Vitali, *Morandi - Catalogo generale*, 2 vol., Electa, Milan, 1977; 2nd edition updated, Milan, 1983.

G. Giuffré, *Giorgio Morandi*, "I maestri del Novecento", Sansoni, Florence, 1977.

F. Solmi, *Morandi: storia e leggenda*, Grafis, Bologna, 1978.

W. Hertzsch, *Giorgio Morandi*, Seeman, Leipzig, 1979.

L. Martì, *I geni della pittura: Giorgio Morandi*, Armando Curcio, Rome, 1979.

M. Valsecchi, G. Ruggeri, *Morandi - Disegni*, vol. I (E. Tavoni ed.), La Casa dell'Arte, Sasso Marconi, 1981.

G. Soavi, *La polvere di Morandi*, Officine Grafiche Elli & Pagani, Milan, 1982.

J. Jouvet, W. Schmied, *Giorgio Morandi - Olbider, Aquarelle, Zeichnungen, Radierungen*, Diogenes, Zurich, 1982.

L. Magnani, *Il mio Morandi*, Einaudi, Turin, 1982.

F. Basile, *Il laboratorio della solitudine*, La Casa dell'Arte, Sasso Marconi, 1982.

C.L. Ragghianti, *Bologna cruciale 1914 e saggi su Morandi, Gorni, Saetti*, Calderini, Bologna, 1982.

C. Brandi, *Giorgio Morandi - Seine Werke im Morat-Institut für Kunstwissenschaft*, Morat-Institut, Fribourg, 1984.

G.C. Argan, F. Basile, *Morandi - Disegni*, vol. II (E. Tavoni ed.), La Casa dell'Arte, Sasso Marconi, 1984.

G. Briganti, E. Coen, *I paesaggi di Morandi*, Umberto Allemandi, Turin, 1984.

M. Prisco, "Morandi inedito," in *Prova d'Autore*, monographic issue, I, no. 1, 1984.

J.-M. Folon, *Fiori di Giorgio Morandi* (with a poem by G. Testori), Alice, Geneva, and Biti, Milan, 1985.

F. Solmi, *Morandi alla Galleria Comunale d'Arte Moderna di Bologna* (scientific contribution of M. Pasquali), Grafis, Bologna, 1985.

Morandi e il suo tempo, Mazzotta, Milan, 1985.

*I Incontro internazionale di studi su Giorgio Morandi - "Morandi e il suo tempo" - Qua-*derni morandiani 1, Mazzotta, Milan, 1985.

Morandi - 100 opere su carta - Acquarelli, di-segni e acqueforti, Mazzotta, Milan, 1985.

Exhibitions

by Marilena Pasquali

1914
Bologna, Hôtel Baglioni, 21-22 March (with O. Licini, M. Bacchelli, S. Pozzati, G. Vespignani).
Rome, Palazzo delle Esposizioni, spring. II Esposizione internazionale della Secessione.
Rome, Galleria Sprovieri, 3 April - 15 May: I Esposizione libera futurista.

1917
Lugo, Scuole Comunali, November: Esposizione d'arte interregionale.

1921
Berlin, Staatliche Kunsthalle, March: Mostra di "Valori Plastici" (traveled to Dresden, Hanover and Munich).

1922
Florence, Palazzo Sangallo, 8 April - 31 July: La Fiorentina primaverile.

1926
Milan, Palazzo della Permanente, February-March: I Mostra del Novecento italiano.
Florence, Stanze del "Selvaggio," February-March: I Mostra d'arte del gruppo del "Selvaggio."

1927
Florence, April: II Esposizione internazionale dell'incisione moderna.

1928
Venice: XVI Esposizione biennale internazionale d'arte.

1929
Milan, Palazzo della Permanente, March-April: II Mostra del Novecento italiano.
Pittsburgh: XXVIII Carnegie Award.
Paris, Galerie Bonaparte, 30 November - 20 December: Exposition d'art italien moderne.

1930
Basel, Kunsthalle, 5 January - 2 February: Moderne Italiener.
Bern, Kunsthalle Bern, 16 March - 4 May: Artisti della nuova Italia.
Venice: XVII Esposizione biennale internazionale d'arte.
Paris, Bibliothèque Nationale, November: Exposition de la gravure et de la médaille italienne contemporaine.
Buenos Aires: 20th-Century Italian Art.
Pittsburgh: XXIX Carnegie Award.

1931
Rome, Palazzo delle Esposizioni, January-June: I Quadriennale d'arte nazionale.
Athens, 26 April - 3 May: Italian Week in Athens.

1932
Florence, IV Fiera internazionale del libro: I Mostra dell'incisione italiana moderna.

Paris, Galerie Georges Bernheim, 4-19 March: Artistes italiens modernes.

1933
Vienna, Künstlerhaus, 1 April - 5 June: Moderne italienische Kunst.
Pittsburgh, 19 October - 10 December: XXXI Carnegie Award.

1934
Venice: XIX Esposizione biennale internazionale d'arte.
United States: Exhibition of Contemporary Italian Painting.

1935
Rome, Palazzo delle Esposizioni, February-July: II Quadriennale d'arte nazionale.
Paris, Musée du Jeu de Paume, May-July: L'art italien des XIXe et XXe siècles.

1936
Paris, Universal Exhibition, Italian pavilion: group show.
Pittsburgh, 15 October - 6 December: The 1936 International Exhibition of Painting.

1937
Rome, Galleria di Roma: opening exhibition.
Berlin: Italian Art Exhibition.
New York, Cometa Art Gallery: Anthology of Contemporary Italian Drawing.

New York, Cometa Art Gallery: Anthology of Contemporary Italian Painting.

1938
Bern, Kunsthalle, October: Ausstellung der Moderner italienische Kunst.

1939
Rome, Palazzo delle Esposizioni, February-July: III Quadriennale d'arte nazionale.
San Francisco, Golden Gate: Golden Gate International Exhibition of Contemporary Art.
Kaunas: Exhibition of engravings.

1940
Zurich: Italian Art Exhibition.

1941
Cortina d'Ampezzo: Mostra del collezionista (first prize awarded to the artist).

1942
Bologna, Galleria Ciangottini, April: Italian Masters Exhibition.
Milan, Pinacoteca di Brera, 7-22 November: Mostra della collezione Pietro Feroldi.

1943
Rome, Palazzo delle Esposizioni, May-July: IV Quadriennale d'arte nazionale.
Venice, Galleria del Cavallino, November: one-man exhibition of graphic works.

1945
Florence, Galleria del Fiore, 21 April - 3 May: one-man exhibition.
Rome, Galleria La Palma: April-May: one-man exhibition.
Como, Galleria Borromini: Pittura contemporanea.

1946
Modena, Sala delle Mostre dell'Università, 24 February - 3 March: Maestri della pittura contemporanea.
Rome, Galleria dell'Obelisco, November: one-man exhibition.
Milano, Circolo delle Grazie: one-man exhibition.

1947
Rio de Janeiro, Ministry of Public Education, May: Modern Italian Painting.
Pisa, Palazzo alla Giornata, July-August: Mostra di pittura italiana contemporanea.

1948
Rome, Galleria Nazionale d'Arte Moderna, March-May: Rassegna nazionale di arti figurative.
Venice, 29 May - 30 September: XXIV Esposizione biennale internazionale d'arte.
Venice, Galleria del Cavallino, 14 June: one-man exhibition.
Stockholm, Färg och Form, September: Italiensk Nutdskonst.
Göteborg, Konstmuseet, October: Italiensk Nutdskonst.
Rome, Calcografia Nazionale, autumn: anthology of graphic works.

1949
Catania, February-April: Mostra d'arte contemporanea (Quarant'anni d'arte italiana).
Cairo, Palais Ismail Pacha, February-March: Exposition de peinture moderne italienne depuis 1850 jusqu'à nos jours.
Milan, Politecnico, 9-16 April: Mostra organizzata dall'Associazione studenti universitari.
Brussels, Palais des Beaux-Arts, May-June: one-man exhibition of graphic works.
Salsomaggiore, Grand Hotel des Termes, May-June: Cinquant'anni di pittura italiana.
New York, Museum of Modern Art, 28 June - 18 September: Twentieth-Century Italian Art.
Vienna, Akademie der Bildenden Künste, 10 December 1949 - 10 January 1950: Italienische Malerei der Gegenwart.
Milan, Galleria dell'Annunciata, December 1949 - January 1950: one-man exhibition.

1950
Brussels, Palais des Beaux-Arts, 28 January - 26 February: Art italien contemporain.
Amsterdam, Stedelijk Museum, 3 March - 3 May: Figuren uit de Italiaanse Schilderkunst na 1910.
Paris, Musée National d'Art Moderne, May-June: Exposition d'art moderne italien.
London, Tate Gallery, 25 June - 31 July: Exhibition of Modern Italian Art.
Zurich, Kunsthaus, November-December: Futurismo e pittura metafisica.
Lugano: I Mostra internazionale del bianco e nero (award for etching).
Copenhagen: Exhibition of Modern Italian Painting.

1951
Cincinnati, Cincinnati Art Museum, 2 February - 4 March: Paintings 1900-1925.
Helsinki, Konsthallen, March: Esposizione d'arte italiana contemporanea (traveled to Oslo, Kunsternes Hus; Copenhagen, Frie Udstilling; Göteborg, Konsthallen).
Lordgen, 14 April: Grafik av Giorgio Morandi (with Carlo Carrà).
Salerno, Galleria Il Setaccio, 9 July: one-man exhibition.
Turin, Palazzo delle Belle Arti - Parco del Valentino, October: I Mostra Italia-Francia - Pittori d'oggi.
São Paulo, Museu de Arte Moderna, October-December: I Bienal / Artistas italianos de hoje.
Brussels: Italian Art Printing.
The Hague, Gemeentemuseum: Drie Grafici.

1952
Paris, Musée National d'Art Moderne, March: Jeune gravure contemporaine.
Venice, 14 June - 19 October: XXVI Esposizione biennale internazionale d'arte.
Pittsburgh, Carnegie Institute, 16 October - 14 December: The 1952 Pittsburgh International Exhibition of Contemporary Painting.

1953
Stockholm, Liljevalchs Konsthall, 6 March - 12 April: Italiensk Nutdskonst.
Florence, Palazzo Strozzi, April-May: Arte moderna in una raccolta italiana.
São Paulo, Museu de Arte Moderna, October-December: II Bienal (award for engraving).

1954
The Hague, Gemeentemuseum, 14 April - 6 June: anthology of works (traveled to Rotterdam).
London, New Burlington Galleries, 25 June - 24 July: anthology of works.
Hamburg, Kunsthalle, June-July (traveled to Cologne, Istituto italiano di Cultura).
Milan, Palazzo Reale, November 1954 - February 1955: 103 dipinti del Museo d'arte di San Paolo del Brasile.

1955
London, Institute of Contemporary Art, 9 June - 2 July: Twentieth-Century Paintings and Sculptures.
Kassel, Museum Friedricianum, I Docu-

menta 1955, 15 July - 18 September: Kunst des XX. Jahrhunderts.
New York, Delius Gallery, 4 October - 5 November: one-man exhibition.
Rome, Galleria La Medusa, 29 October: one-man exhibition.
Rome, Palazzo delle Esposizioni, November 1955 - April 1956: VII Quadriennale nazionale d'arte: Antologia della pittura e scultura italiane dal 1910 al 1930.

1956
New York, John Heller Gallery, January-February: Giorgio Morandi, Massimo Campigli, Anton Music.
New York, Columbus Gallery of Fine Arts, 9 March - 15 April: Italian Design Today.
Winterthur, Kunstmuseum, 24 June - 29 July: Giorgio Morandi/Giacomo Manzù.
Deerfield, Deerfield Academy, 20 October - 10 November: Contemporary Italian Art.
London, Tate Gallery, 21 November - 19 December: Modern Italian Art from the Estorick Collection.
Zagreb, Ljubljana, Skoplje, Belgrade, October 1956 - January 1957: Exhibition of Contemporary Italian Art.

1957
Plymouth, City Museum & Art Gallery, 26 January - 16 February: Modern Italian Art from the Estorick Collection.
Birmingham, City Museum & Art Gallery, 23 February - 16 March: Modern Italian Art from the Estorick Collection.
Ivrea, Centro Culturale Canavesano, March: L'opera grafica.
Turin, Galleria Galatea, May: one-man exhibition.
Munich, Haus der Kunst, 7 June - 15 September: Kunstausstellung München 1957 und Ausstellung italienischer Kunst von 1910 bis zur Gegenwart.
São Paulo, Museu de Arte Moderna, September-December: IV Bienal (award for painting).
New York, World House Gallery, 5 November - 7 December: Giorgio Morandi / Retrospective 1912-1957.
South America, Diez años de pintura italiana - Traveling exhibition in South America organized by the Venice Biennale on behalf of the Ministry of Foreign Affairs and the Ministry of Public Education.

1958
New York, The American Federation of Art, February-June: Manzù and Morandi.
Lugano, 3 April - 15 June: V Mostra internazionale di bianco e nero (award for engraving).
Brussels, Palais des Beaux-Arts, 17 April - 21 July: 50 ans d'art moderne.
Lincoln (Mass.), De Cordoba Museum, 27 April - 1 June: A Decade in Review.
Caracas, Galeria de Arte Contemporáneo, September: Morandi, Tosi, Marino Marini, Campigli, Sironi, de Pisis.
Turin, Galleria Galatea, October: Disegni e incisioni di Morandi, Casorati e Spazzapan.
Pittsburgh, Carnegie Institute, 5 December 1958 - 8 February 1959: 1896/1955 - Retrospective Exhibition of Paintings from Previous International.
Copenhagen, Charlottenborg Palace: Exhibition of Modern Italian Art.

1959
Padua, Galleria Le Stagioni, January: 30 etchings.
St. Etienne, Musée d'Art et d'Industrie, May: Peintres et sculpteurs italiens du futurisme à nos jours (traveled to Dijon, July; Blois, September; Lyon, October; Charleroi, December).
Rome, Palazzo Barberini, 4 June - 6 September: Il futurismo.
Kassel, Museum Friedricianum, II Documenta 1959, 11 July - 11 October: Kunst nach 1945.
Winterthur, Kunst Museum, 4 October - 15 November: Exhibition of Futurist Art.
Turin, Galleria Civica d'Arte Moderna, 31 October - 8 December: Capolavori d'arte moderna nelle collezioni private.
Milan, Galleria dell'Annunciata, December 1959 - January 1960: one-man exhibition.

1960
Milan, Palazzo Reale, April-June: Arte italiana del XX secolo da collezioni americane.
New York, N. Knoedler & Co., 12 April - 14 May: The Colin Collection.
Boston, Boston University Art Gallery, 23 April - 14 May: Works from Private Collections.
Ancona, Palazzo del Liceo Scientifico, 3-24 July: Premio Marche '60.
Luzern, Kunstmuseum, 6 August - 18 September: Italienische Maler der Gegenwart.
Paris, Musée National d'Art Moderne, 4 November - 23 January 1961: Les arts en Europe de 1884 à 1914.
New York, World House Galleries, 6 December 1960 - 14 January 1961: one-man exhibition.

1961
New York, The Museum of Modern Art, February: The James Thrall Soby Collection.
Chicago, Illinois Institute of Technology, 5-30 April: The Maremont Collection of Twentieth Century.
Amsterdam, Stedelijk Museum, 22 August - 8 September: Polarities: the Dionysian and the Apollonian in Art.
Turin, Italia '61: Da Boldini a Pollock (traveled to Milan, Padiglione d'Arte Contemporanea).

1962
Venice, Ca' Pesaro, XXXI Biennale internazionale d'arte, 16 June - 7 October: Mostra dei grandi premi della Biennale 1948-60.
Siegen, Haus seel am Markt, 27 October - 17 November: Giorgio Morandi Rubenspreis 1962 der Stadt Siegen.
Milan, Galleria Galatea, December: one-man exhibition of etchings.
Philadelphia, Philadelphia Museum of Art.
Milan, Galleria Lorenzelli, December 1962 - January 1963: Mostra Magini-Morandi.

1963
Naples, Galleria Il Centro, January-February: 40 incisioni di Giorgio Morandi.
Paris, Grand Palais, 22 May - 3 June: Art contemporain.
Strasbourg, Musée des Beaux-Arts, June-September: La grande aventure de l'art du XXᵉ siècle.
Viareggio, Galleria Nettuno, July: L'opera grafica di Giorgio Morandi.
Hamburg, Kunstverein, 28 September - 3 November: Italien 1905-1925: Futurismus und Pittura metafisica.
Beirut, Istituto Italiano di Cultura, October-November: Dipinti italiani d'oggi.
Rome, Galleria L'Obelisco, November: one-man exhibition.
Ginevra, Galerie Krugier, November: one-man exhibition.
New York, Marlborough-Gerson Gallery, 2 November - 21 December: Artist and Maecenas / A Tribute to Curt Valentin.
Washington, National Gallery of Art, 16

December 1963 - 1 March 1964: Paintings from the Museum of Modern Art, New York.

1964
Zurich, Galerie Obere Zäune, March: one-man exhibition of graphic works.
Washington, Washington Gallery of Modern Art, 1 April - 3 May: Treasures of Twentieth-Century Art from the Maremont Collection.
Bielefeld, Städtisches Kunsthaus, April-May: one-man exhibition.
London, Tate Gallery, 22 April - 28 June: Exhibitions 54-64 / Painting and Sculpture of a Decade.
Lausanne, Palais de Beaulieu, 1 May - 24 October: Chefs-d'œuvres des collections suisses de Manet à Picasso.
Caracas, Fundación Eugenio Mendoza, 17-31 May: Preferencias de los coleccionistas.
Venice, XXXII Esposizione biennale internazionale d'arte, May-September: Arte d'oggi nei musei.
Karlsruhe, Badischer Kunstverein, 22 June - 26 July: one-man exhibition.
Baltimore, Museum of Art, 1 August - 15 November: Exhibition for the museum's fiftieth anniversary.
Ancona, 6-29 September: Premio Marche '64 - Omaggio a Giorgio Morandi.
Munich, Galerie Atelier Monpti, September-October: one-man exhibition.
Milan, Galleria delle Ore, October: Omaggio a Morandi.
Munich, Atelier Monpti, October: retrospective exhibition.
Naples, Palazzo Reale, October-November: La natura morta italiana.
Pittsburgh, Museum of Art, Carnegie Institute, 30 October 1964 - 10 January 1965: Pittsburgh International 1964: Exhibition of Contemporary Painting and Sculpture.
Hanover, Kestner-Gesellschaft, November-December: Giorgio Morandi, Alfred Kubin.
Zurich, Kunsthaus, December 1964 - February 1965: La natura morta italiana.

1965
Bologna, Galleria La Loggia, January: Giorgio Morandi and Felice Casorati.
Wupperthal, Kunst und Museumverein, 12 February - 14 March: one-man exhibition.
Rotterdam, Boymans-van Beuningen Museum, March-April: La natura morta italiana.

Milan, Galleria Annunciata, April-May: one-man exhibition.
Rome, Galleria La Medusa, May: Marini-Morandi.
Edinburgh, Scottish National Gallery of Modern Art, August-September: The Collections of Works by Giorgio Morandi 1890-1964 Belonging to Professor Luigi Magnani.
Bern, Kunsthalle, 23 October - 5 December: anthology.
Rome, Palazzo delle Esposizioni, October 1965 - March 1966: IX Quadriennale nazionale d'arte.
Caracas, Fundación Mendoza, 1 November - 15 December: Omaggio a Giorgio Morandi.

1966
Milan, Salone dell'Annunciata, January: Maestri del disegno.
Florence, Galleria L'Indiano, March-April: Omaggio a Morandi.
Rome, Galleria Nazionale d'Arte Moderna, 27 March - 25 April: Giorgio Morandi / Opere della collezione Ingrao.
Rome, Calcografia Nazionale, April: Giorgio Morandi - Mostra delle acqueforti.
New York, Public Education Association, 26 April - 21 May: Seven Decades 1895-1965.
Irvine, University of California Art Gallery, 17 May - 10 June: Five Europeans: Bacon, Balthus, Dubuffet, Giacometti, Morandi.
Recklinghausen, Städtisches Museum, 31 May - 23 August: Variationen über ein Thema.
Venice, XXXIII Esposizione biennale internazionale d'arte, 18 June - 16 October: one-man exhibition.
Grizzana, Scuole Comunali, July-August: Omaggio a Giorgio Morandi.
Bologna, Palazzo dell'Archiginnasio, 30 October - 15 December: anthology.
Turin, Galleria La Minima, October-November: Omaggio a Morandi.

1967
Milan, Galleria Ciranna, February-March: Il paesaggio nell'acquaforte di Morandi.
Florence, Palazzo Strozzi, February-May: Arte moderna in Italia 1915-1935.
Milan, Palazzo della Permanente, March: I Mostra d'arte moderna e trame contemporanee.
Ferrara, Galleria Duca d'Este, May: Dise-

gni di Morandi.
New Haven, Yale University Art Gallery, 4 May - 18 June: The Helen and Robert M. Benjamin Collection.
Monza, Galleria Civica, 8-21 June: Esempi di pittura italiana contemporanea.
Padua, Galleria La Chiocciola, November-December: Manzù, Morandi, Marino.
Washington, The Phillips Collection, 30 November 1967 - 11 January 1968: Masters of Italian Art from the Collection of Gianni Mattioli.
Turin, Galleria Civica d'Arte Moderna, November 1967 - January 1968: Le muse inquietanti - Maestri del surrealismo.
Guatemala, Honduras, Salvador, Nicaragua, Costa Rica, July-December: Arte italiano contemporáneo - Traveling exhibition organized by the Rome Quadriennale.

1968
Harvard, Busch-Reisinger Museum Harvard University, 12 January - 10 February: one-man exhibition.
Turin, Galleria Civica d'Arte Moderna, 1 February - 17 March: I pittori italiani dell'Associazione internazionale arti plastiche Unesco.
Dallas, Dallas Museum of Fine Arts, 1 February - 3 March: Masters of Italian Art from the Collection of Gianni Mattioli (traveled to Detroit, 19 June - 21 July; Kansas City, 6 October - 17 November).
San Francisco, San Francisco Museum of Modern Art, 16 March - 21 April: Masters of Italian Art from the Collection of Gianni Mattioli.
Northampton, Smith College Museum of Art, 11-28 April: An Exhibition in Honour of Henry Russel-Hitchcock - 19th and 20th Century.
Brescia, Associazione Artisti Bresciani, April: Incisioni di Giorgio Morandi.
Stuttgart, Galerie Lutz & Meyer, May: one-man exhibition.
Zagreb, Galerija Moderne Umjetnosti, 2-15 May: Bolonjsko Slikarstvo XX Vijeka.
Copenhagen, Kunstforeningen, September: anthology.
Geneva, Galerie Krugier, October-November: one-man exhibition.
Bologna, Galleria de' Foscherari, October-November: Giorgio Morandi - 75 acquarelli dal 1915 al 1963.
Paris, Galerie Villand & Galanis, December 1968 - January 1969: one-man exhibition.

1969

New York, Olivetti, 500 Park Avenue, 5-30 March: Masters of Modern Art from the Collection of Gianni Mattioli (traveled to Boston, 23 January - 23 February 1970).
Milan, Galleria del Milione, March: Testimonianza per Morandi.
Brussels, Palais des Beaux-Arts, 9 September - 12 October: Maîtres de l'art moderne en Italie 1910-1935 - Collection Gianni Mattioli.
Haarlem, Frans Halsmuseum, 6 October - 1 December: Modern Italian Art from Dutch Collections.
Copenhagen, Louisiana Kunstmuseet, 8 November - 14 December: Italiensk Kunst 1910-1935 - Gianni Mattioli Samling.
Cortina d'Ampezzo, Centro d'Arte Dolomiti, 24 December 1969 - 10 January 1970: Omaggio a Giorgio Morandi.

1970

Hamburg, Hamburger Kunsthalle, 19 February - 30 March: Italienische Kunst - Sammlung Gianni Mattioli.
Bologna, Museo Civico, April-May: Due decenni di acquisizioni nelle raccolte comunali d'arte.
Strasbourg, Château de Rohan, 14 May - 15 September: Exposition d'art moderne européen.
Rome, Galleria Don Chisciotte, June: 33 acqueforti.
Bologna, Palazzo dell'Archiginnasio, 12 September - 22 November: Natura ed espressione nell'arte bolognese-emiliana.
Madrid, Museo Español de Arte Contemporaneo, November-December: Maestros del arte moderno en Italia 1910-1935 - Collección Gianni Mattioli (traveled to Barcelona, December 1970 - January 1971).
Berkeley, University Art Museum, University of California, 6 November 1970 - 10 January 1971: Excellence - Art from the University Community.
London, Royal Academy of Art, 5 December 1970 - 17 January 1971: anthology.
Milan, Galleria del Milione, December 1970 - January 1971: Morandi and Morlotti.
Rome, Il Nuovo Torcoliere, December 1970 - January 1971: L'opera grafica di Giorgio Morandi (48 incisioni).
Cortina d'Ampezzo, Galleria Dolomiti: one-man exhibition.

1971

Seville, Museo de Arte Contemporáneo, January-February: Maestros del arte moderno en Italia 1910-1935 - Collección Gianni Mattioli.
Paris, Musée National d'Art Moderne, 9 February - 12 April: anthology.
Milan, Palazzo della Permanente: March-May: Mostra di pittori e scultori che recitano a soggetto.
Milan, Rotonda della Besana, May-June: anthology.
Milan, Galleria Annunciata, June-July: one-man exhibition.
Vicenza, Palazzo Chiericati, 4-26 September: L'arte moderna nel collezionismo vicentino.
Berlin, Nationalgalerie, 11 September - 7 November: Metamorfosi dell'oggetto.
Turin, Galleria Dantesca, December 1971 - January 1972: one-man exhibition.

1972

Amsterdam, Stedelijk Museum, January-February: Morandi-Etsen.
Milan, Palazzo Reale, 17 January - 23 February: Metamorfosi dell'oggetto.
Kyoto, National Museum of Modern Art, 15 April - 21 May: Masters of Modern Italian Art (traveled to Tokyo, 31 May - 2 July).
Milan, Galleria Eunomia, May-June: one-man exhibition.
Boston, Museum of Fine Arts, 8 June - 8 October: The Rathbone Years.
Venice, Museo Correr, XXXVI Esposizione biennale internazionale d'arte, 11 June - 1 October: Capolavori della pittura del XX secolo, 1900-1945.
Rome, Palazzo delle Esposizioni, November 1972 - May 1973: X Quadriennale d'arte nazionale.

1973

Leningrad, Ermitage, 17 April - 10 May: anthology (traveled to Moscow, Puskin Museum, 18 May - 16 June).
Rome, Galleria Nazionale d'Arte Moderna, 18 May - 22 July: antologica.
Paris, Musée des Arts Décoratifs, May-June: 1928-1973 - Domus, 45 anni di architettura, design, arte.
Urbino, Palazzo Ducale, June-July: Le acqueforti di Giorgio Morandi.
Geneva, Musée Rath, 28 June - 23 September: Art du XXᵉ siècle - Collections genevoises.

Frankfurt, Frankfurter Westend Galerie, October-November: one-man exhibition.

1974

Milan, Palazzo Reale, 27 May - 20 September: 50 anni di pittura italiana nella collezione Boschi-Di Stefano donata al Comune di Milano.
Karlsruhe, Badischer Kunstverein, 22 June - 26 July: anthology.

1975

Bologna, Galleria Comunale d'Arte Moderna, May-June: anthology.
Darmstadt, Kunsthalle, 24 May - 6 July: Realismus und Realität - Ausstellung zum 11. Darmstäder Gespräch.
Lugano, Villa Malpensata, 28 August - 9 November: Dalle collezioni d'arte private ticinesi; maestri europei del XX secolo.

1976

Bologna, Galleria Marescalchi, May: Omaggio a Morandi.
Bologna, Galleria Due Torri, May: Un confronto: due tempi, Licini-Morandi.
Verona, Galleria dello Scudo, November 1976 - January 1977: one-man exhibition.

1977

Berlin, Kunstausstellung, 14 August - 16 October: Tendenzen der Zwanziger Jahre.
Vancouver, The Vancouver Art Gallery, October: anthology.
Lucca, Galleria Barsotti, October: one-man exhibition.
Sasso Marconi, Casa dell'Arte, October-November: one-man exhibition.
Geneva, Galerie Jeanneret, November 1977 - January 1978: one-man exhibition.

1978

Bologna, Galleria Comunale d'Arte Moderna, June-September: Metafisica del quotidiano.
Ferrara, Palazzo dei Diamanti - Galleria Civica d'Arte Moderna, July-October: anthology.

1979

Paris, Galerie Berggruen, February: Les eauxfortes de Giorgio Morandi.
Milan, Padiglione d'Arte Contemporanea: Miti del Novecento.
Venice, Palazzo Grassi, May: La pittura metafisica.
Bordeaux, Musée des Beaux-Arts: anthol-

ogy of graphic works.
Milan, Palazzo Reale, October 1979 - January 1980: Origini dell'astrattismo - Verso nuovi orizzonti del reale.

1980
Rome, Galleria Il Gabbiano, March-April: one-man exhibition.
Bologna, Galleria Comunale d'Arte Moderna, May-August: La metafisica - Gli anni Venti.
Focette di Marina di Pietrasanta, Galleria Farsetti, July-August: one-man exhibition.
Cavalese, Casa dell'Arte, July-August: one-man exhibition.
Bologna, Galleria Trimarchi, December: Giorgio Morandi - Disegni.
Paris, Centre Georges Pompidou, December 1980 - April 1981: Les réalismes (traveled to Berlin, Staatliche Kunsthalle, May-June 1981).

1981
Sasso Marconi, Casa dell'Arte, May: one-man exhibition.
Munich, Haus der Kunst, 18 June - 6 September: anthology.
Acqui Terme, Palazzo Saracco, July-September: anthology.
Vevey, Musée des Beaux-Arts, August-October: Les peintres du silence.
San Francisco, Museum of Modern Art, 24 September - 1 November: anthology organized by the Des Moines Art Center (traveled to New York, The Solomon R. Guggenheim Museum, 19 November 1981 - 17 January 1982; Des Moines, Des Moines Art Center, 1 February - 14 March 1981).
Florence, Galleria Santa Croce, October: one-man exhibition.
Cellatica (Brescia), October-November: Il linguaggio dell'incisione (traveled to Capo di Ponte, November-December; Trieste and Innsbruck, spring 1982).
Frankfurt, Frankfurter Westend Galerie: Zur italienischen Kunst nach 1945 - Deutsche Künstler und Italien.
Norrbottens, Norrbottens Museum, October 1981 - April 1982: one-man exhibition.

1982
Venice-Mestre, Galleria Plus Art, January: Disegni e acqueforti di Giorgio Morandi.
Milan, Palazzo Reale, 27 January - 30 April: Gli anni Trenta - Arte e cultura in Italia.
Bologna, Galleria Comunale d'Arte Moder-

na, February-March: La scuola bolognese dell'acquaforte.
Bologna, Galleria Comunale d'Arte Moderna, from May: Morandi in Galleria - Opere e documenti (permanent space).
Turin, Teatro Regio, November: Mostra della Fondazione Guido ed Ettore De Fornariis.

1983
Zagreb, Graphics Department of the Yugoslav Academy of Sciences and Fine Arts January: Etchings by di Giorgio Morandi (traveled to Rijeka, Galerija Moderna, February).
Milan, Palazzo della Permanente, January-March: Mostra del Novecento italiano.
Modena, Galleria Civica, 28 July - 15 October: Disegno italiano fra le due guerre.
New York, Solomon R. Guggenheim Museum: Aspects of Postwar Painting in Europe.
Mamiano di Parma, Fondazione Magnani-Rocca, September-October: Da Cézanne a Morandi e oltre.
Parma, Centro Steccata, November: Disegni e incisioni di Giorgio Morandi.

1984
Sasso Marconi, Casa dell'Arte, January-March: anthology.
Washington, Hirshhorn Museum - Smithsonian Institution, February-April: Contemporary Italian Art.
Bologna, Pinacoteca Nazionale, from 26 April: Giorgio Morandi - 10 quadri in Pinacoteca.
Freiburg im Breisgau, Morat-Institut für Kunst und Kunstwissenschaft, May: Morat-Institut collection permanent space.
Rome, Galleria Mara Coccia, May: Morandi - Disegni 1915-1963.
Sorrento, Istituto Statale d'Arte, May-June: Omaggio a Giorgio Morandi a vent'anni dalla morte (exhibition of photographs in collaboration with the Galleria Comunale d'Arte Moderna di Bologna).
Cardiff, National Museum of Wales, October - November: Bolognese Etching (traveled to Brecon, Brecknock Museum, 24 November - 22 December; Carmarthen, Carmarthen County Museum, 5 January - 2 February 1985; Llanelly, Llanelly Library, February-March 1985; Newcastle, University Art Gallery, March-April 1985): in collaboration with the Galleria Comunale d'Arte Moderna of Bologna.

Rome, Galleria La Tartaruga, November: Giorgio Morandi - 60 acqueforti.
Venice, Opera Bevilacqua La Masa, November: Opere degli artisti premiati dal 1947 al 1967.
Milan, Rotonda della Besana, November-December: Gli scrittori presentano i pittori.
Rome, Galleria dell'Oca, November 1984 - 30 January 1985: I paesaggi di Morandi.
Madrid, Sala de Exposiciones - Caja de Pensiones, December 1984 - January 1985: anthology (traveled to Barcelona, Caja de Pensiones, February-March 1985; Marseille, Musée Cantini, May-June 1985).

1985
Frankfurt, Frankfurter Kunstverein, February-April: Italienische Kunst 1900-1980 - Hauptwerke aus dem Museo d'Arte Contemporanea, Mailand.
Florence, Gabinetto dei Disegni e delle Stampe degli Uffizi, February: Dieci anni di acquisizioni - 1974-1984.
Sasso Marconi, Casa dell'Arte, April: I giganti del bulino - Morandi, Bartolini, Viviani.
Bologna, Galleria La Loggia, April: Morandi incisore; then Bologna, Pinacoteca Nazionale, May.
Toulouse, Musée des Augustins, April-May: La scuola dell'acquaforte a Bologna.
Florence, Galleria Palazzo Vecchio, October: one-man exhibition.
Salerno, Galleria Il Catalogo, November: one-man exhibition.
Bologna, Galleria Comunale d'Arte Moderna, November 1985 - February 1986: Morandi e il suo tempo.
Milan, Pinacoteca Nazionale di Brera, November 1985 - February 1986; Morandi - 100 opere su carta (traveled to Bologna, Galleria Comunale d'Arte Moderna, February-April 1986).

1986
Ravenna, Loggetta Lombardesca, March-April: Il fantasma della qualità.
Reggio Emilia, Galleria La Scaletta, April: Il disegno italiano.
Sasso Marconi, La Casa dell'Arte, May: Quadrangolo.
Cortona, Palazzo Casali, June: La collezione Timpanaro - Grafica italiana del Novecento.
Venice, XLII Esposizione biennale internazionale d'arte, June-September: Il colore.

Venice, Ca' Corner della Regina, June-September: I premi della Biennale di Venezia.
Valdagno, Villa Marzotto, summer: 1951-1968 - I premi Marzotto.
Mesola, Castello Estense, July-September: Paesaggio senza territorio.
Turin, Palazzina della Società Promotrice delle Belle Arti, November 1986 - January 1987: Arte moderna a Torino.
Bari, Pinacoteca Provinciale, December 1986: La collezione Grieco.

Bologna, Galleria La Loggia, December: Artisti bolognesi nell'incisione.
New York, Casa Italiana - Center for Italian Studies of Columbia University, December: Italics - 1925-1985: Sessant'anni di vita culturale in Italia (organized by the Istituto dell'Enciclopedia Italiana).
Cortina d'Ampezzo, Galleria Marescalchi, December 1986 - February 1987: one-man exhibition.
Florence, Galleria d'Arte Moderna di Palazzo Pitti, December 1986 - June 1987: Le collezioni del Novecento - 1915-1945.

1987
Rome, Galleria dell'Oca, January: De Pisis, Morandi, Sironi.
Rome, Galleria Nazionale d'Arte Moderna, February: opening of the 20th-century rooms.
Rome, Palazzo delle Esposizioni, June-September: Le "Secessioni" romane.
Paris, Hôtel de Ville, June-August: anthology.

Catalogue of Works

Paintings

1. *Landscape*, 1911.
Oil on paste-board, 14³/4 × 20¹/2 in.
Dated lower right: 6.911.
Private collection, Milan.

2. *Portrait of Woman*, n.d. (1912).
Oil on canvas, 17¹/2 × 14⁵/8 in.
Private collection, Bologna.

3. *Nude*, 1914.
Oil on canvas, 26 × 11⁷/8 in.
Signed and dated lower right: Morandi /
1914.
Mattioli Collection, Milan.

4. *Still Life*, 1914.
Oil on canvas, 39¹/2 × 15³/4 in.
Signed and dated lower left: Morandi /
914.
Musée National d'Art Moderne, Paris.

5. *Landscape*, 1914.
Oil on canvas, 23 × 19¹/4 in.
Signed and dated lower right: Morandi,
1914.
Mattioli Collection, Milan.

6. *Still Life*, 1915.
Oil on canvas, 29¹/4 × 53⁷/8 in.
Signed and dated lower left: Morandi
1915.
Mattioli Collection, Milan.

7. *Flowers*, 1916.
Tempera on board, 23⁵/8 × 19⁵/8 in.
Pinacoteca Nazionale di Brera (Gift of
Emilio and Maria Jesi), Milan.

8. *Still Life*, 1916.
Oil on canvas, 23⁵/8 × 21¹/4 in.
Signed lower right: Morandi. Dated on ver-
so: 1916.
Mattioli Collection, Milan.

9. *Still Life*, 1919.
Oil on canvas, 21 × 22⁵/8 in.
Signed and dated upper left: Morandi 919.
Private collection, Milan.

10. *Still Life*, 1918.
Oil on canvas, 27 × 28³/8 in.
Pinacoteca Nazionale di Brera (Gift of
Emilio and Maria Jesi), Milan.

11. *Still Life*, 1919.
Oil on canvas, 22¹/4 × 18¹/2 in.
Signed and dated upper right: Morandi
919.
Pinacoteca Nazionale di Brera (Gift of
Emilio and Maria Jesi), Milan.

12. *Flowers*, 1920.
Oil on canvas, 18¹/8 × 15³/8 in.
Signed and dated lower right: Morandi
920.
Private collection, Milan.

13. *Still Life*, 1920.
Oil on canvas, 23³/4 × 26¹/8 in.
Signed and dated upper center: Morandi
920.
Private collection, Milan.

14. *Still Life*, 1920.
Oil on canvas, 12 × 17¹/2 in.
Signed and dated lower right: Morandi
920.
Galleria Comunale d'Arte Moderna (Gift
of the Morandi sisters), Bologna.

15. *Flowers*, 1924.
Oil on canvas, 22⁷/8 × 18⁷/8 in.
Galleria Comunale d'Arte Moderna (Gift
of the Morandi sisters), Bologna.

16. *Flowers*, 1924.
Oil on canvas, 15 × 16¹/2 in.
Signed and dated upper center: Morandi,
924.
F. Fabbi Collection, Modena.

17. *Self-Portrait*, 1924.
Oil on canvas, 20⁷/8 × 17¹/4 in.
Signed and dated lower center: Morandi
924.
Private collection, Milan.

18. *Garden of Via Fondazza*, 1924.
Oil on canvas, 13 × 16¹/2 in.
Signed on verso: Morandi.
Private collection, Reggio Emilia.

19. *Still Life*, 1929.

Oil on canvas, $20^1/_2 \times 18^1/_2$ in.
Signed on verso: Morandi.
F. Fabbi Collection, Modena.

20. *Still Life*, n.d. (1929).
Oil on canvas, $11^3/_4 \times 23^5/_8$ in.
Private collection, Mestre.

21. *Still Life*, 1929.
Oil on canvas, $21^5/_8 \times 22^1/_2$ in.
Signed and dated on verso: Morandi 1929.
Pinacoteca Nazionale di Brera (Gift of Emilio and Maria Jesi), Milan.

22. *Still Life*, 1929-30.
Oil on canvas, $16^1/_2 \times 19^7/_8$ in.
Private collection, Milan.

23. *Still Life*, 1936.
Oil on canvas, $18^5/_8 \times 23^5/_8$ in.
Galleria Comunale d'Arte Moderna (Gift of the Morandi sisters), Bologna.

24. *Landscape*, 1940.
Oil on canvas, $18^7/_8 \times 16^1/_8$ in.
Signed and dated lower left: Morandi / 1940.
Galleria Comunale d'Arte Moderna (Gnudi bequest), Bologna.

25. *Still Life*, 1941.
Oil on canvas, $16^1/_8 \times 19^1/_2$ in.
Signed and dated lower right: Morandi / 1941.
S. Lodi Collection, Campione d'Italia.

26. *Still Life*, 1941.
Oil on canvas, $17^3/_4 \times 18^1/_2$ in.
Signed lower center: Morandi.
Private collection, Milan.

27. *Flowers*, 1942.
Oil on canvas, $9^7/_8 \times 11^7/_8$ in.
Signed and dated lower left: Morandi / 1942.
F. Fabbi Collection, Modena.

28. *Flowers*, 1942.
Oil on canvas, $11^7/_8 \times 10^1/_4$ in.
Signed and dated lower right: Morandi / 1942.
F. Fabbi Collection, Modena.

29. *Landscape*, 1941.
Oil on canvas, $15^3/_8 \times 18^7/_8$ in.
Signed and dated lower left: Morandi 1941.

Private collection, Milan.

30. *Landscape*, 1942.
Oil on canvas, $10^7/_8 \times 20^1/_2$ in.
Signed on verso: Morandi. Signed and dated on stretcher: Morandi 1942.
G. Salvaterra Collection, Modena.

31. *Landscape*, 1943.
Oil on canvas, $19^1/_4 \times 20^1/_2$ in.
Signed and dated lower left: Morandi 1943.
Private collection, Milan.

32. *Still Life*, 1943.
Oil on canvas, $11^7/_8 \times 17^3/_4$ in.
Signed lower right: Morandi.
F. Fabbi Collection, Modena.

33. *Flowers*, 1946.
Oil on canvas, $9^1/_4 \times 10^5/_8$ in.
Signed lower right: Morandi.
Galleria Comunale d'Arte Moderna (C. Malvasia bequest), Bologna.

34. *Still Life*, 1946.
Oil on canvas, $16 \times 17^7/_8$ in.
Private collection, Milan.

35. *Still Life*, 1948.
Oil on canvas, $14^1/_8 \times 19^5/_8$ in.
Signed lower right: Morandi.
Private collection, Bologna.

36. *Flowers*, 1950.
Oil on canvas, $15^3/_4 \times 13^3/_4$ in.
Signed lower center: Morandi.
Galleria Comunale d'Arte Moderna, Bologna.

37. *Still Life*, 1949.
Oil on canvas, $9^7/_8 \times 13^3/_4$ in.
Galleria Comunale d'Arte Moderna (Gift of the Morandi sisters), Bologna.

38. *Flowers*, 1950.
Oil on canvas, $13^3/_8 \times 10^1/_4$ in.
Signed lower center: Morandi.
Private collection, Milan.

39. *Flowers*, 1950.
Oil on canvas, $14^1/_4 \times 11^7/_8$ in.
Signed lower left: Morandi.
Galleria Comunale d'Arte Moderna, Bologna.

40. *Still Life*, 1951.

Oil on canvas, $14^1/_4 \times 19^5/_8$ in.
Signed lower right: Morandi.
Galleria Comunale d'Arte Moderna, Bologna.

41. *Still Life*, 1952.
Oil on canvas, $12^5/_8 \times 18^7/_8$ in.
Signed lower left: Morandi.
Galleria Comunale d'Arte Moderna, Bologna.

42. *Still Life*, 1955.
Oil on canvas, $13^3/_4 \times 15^3/_4$ in.
Signed lower right: Morandi.
Private collection, Milan.

43. *Still Life*, n.d. (1956).
Oil on canvas, $9^7/_8 \times 15^3/_4$ in.
Signed lower left: Morandi.
Galleria Comunale d'Arte Moderna, Bologna.

44. *Courtyard of Via Fondazza*, 1954.
Oil on canvas, 22×22 in.
Signed lower left: Morandi.
Galleria Comunale d'Arte Moderna, Bologna.

45. *Flowers*, 1957.
Oil on canvas, $11 \times 10^1/_4$ in.
Signed lower center: Morandi.
Galleria Comunale d'Arte Moderna (C. Malvasia bequest), Bologna.

46. *Still Life*, 1956.
Oil on canvas, $11^7/_8 \times 13^3/_4$ in.
Signed lower left: Morandi.
G. Domeniconi Collection, Modena.

47. *Still Life*, 1956.
Oil on canvas, $11^7/_8 \times 17^3/_4$ in.
Signed lower center: Morandi.
Galleria Comunale d'Arte Moderna, Bologna.

48. *Still Life*, 1957.
Oil on canvas, $13^3/_4 \times 16$ in.
Signed lower left: Morandi.
Private collection, Milan.

49. *Still Life*, 1958.
Oil on canvas, $7^7/_8 \times 11^7/_8$ in.
Signed lower left: Morandi.
Galleria Comunale d'Arte Moderna, Bologna.

50. *Still Life*, 1959.
Oil on canvas, $9^7/_8 \times 13^3/_4$ in.

Signed lower left: Morandi.
F. Fabbi Collection, Modena.

51. *Courtyard of Via Fondazza*, 1959.
Oil on canvas, 16 × 17⁷/8 in.
Private collection, Sasso Marconi.

52. *Still Life*, 1960.
Oil on canvas, 13³/4 × 15³/4 in.
Signed lower left: Morandi.
Private collection, Milan.

53. *Still Life*, 1960.
Oil on canvas, 11⁷/8 × 15³/4 in.
Signed lower left: Morandi.
F. Fabbi Collection, Modena.

54. *Still Life*, 1961.
Oil on canvas, 11⁷/8 × 13³/4 in.
Signed lower right: Morandi.
Antonello Trombadori Collection, Rome.

55. *Landscape*, 1962.
Oil on canvas, 19⁵/8 × 19⁵/8 in.
Galleria Comunale d'Arte Moderna (Gift
of Morandi sisters), Bologna.

56. *Landscape*, 1963.
Oil on canvas, 15³/4 × 17³/4 in.
Signed lower center: Morandi.
Galleria Comunale d'Arte Moderna (Gift
of Morandi sisters), Bologna.

57. *Still Life*, 1963.
Oil on canvas, 11⁷/8 × 13³/4 in.
Signed lower left: Morandi.
Private collection, Bologna.

Watercolors

58. *Bather*, 1918.
Watercolor on paper, 8¹/4 × 6¹/4 in.
Signed lower center: Morandi. Dated lower
right: 6 aprile 918.
Private collection, Milan.

59. *Landscape*, n.d. (1956).
Watercolor on paper, 6³/8 × 8¹/4 in.
Signed center: Morandi.
Private collection, Bologna.

60. *Landscape (Interior of Via Fondazza)*,
n.d. (1956).
Watercolor on paper, 8³/8 × 8⁷/8 in.
Signed lower center: Morandi.
Private collection, Verona.

61. *Landscape*, 1958.
Watercolor on paper, 12¹/4 × 8¹/4 in.
Signed and dated lower center: Morandi /
1958.
G. Salvaterra Collection, Modena.

62. *Still Life*, n.d. (1960).
Watercolor on paper, 8¹/4 × 10⁵/8 in.
Signed lower center: Morandi.
Private collection, Verona.

63. *Landscape*, n.d. (1959).
Watercolor on paper, 8¹/4 × 6¹/4 in.
Signed lower center: Morandi.
Private collection, Bologna.

64. *Still Life*, n.d. (1959).
Watercolor on paper, 10⁵/8 × 14¹/2 in.
Signed lower center: Morandi / Morandi.
Private collection, Bologna.

65. *Still Life*, n.d. (1962).
Watercolor on paper, 6¹/4 × 8¹/4 in.
Private collection, Bologna.

66. *Still Life*, n.d. (1962).
Watercolor on paper, 6¹/4 × 8¹/4 in.
Signed lower left: Morandi.
Private collection, Bologna.

Drawings

67. *Still Life*, 1921.
Pencil on paper, 8¹/4 × 12¹/4 in.
Signed and dated lower right: Morandi
921.
Private collection, Milan.

68. *Still Life*, 1928.
Pencil on paper, 10⁵/8 × 15 in.
Signed and dated center: Morandi 1928.
Private collection, Bologna.

69. *Bottles*, 1932.
Pencil on paper, 6³/4 × 9⁵/8 in.
Signed and dated lower center: Morandi
1932.
G. Salvaterra Collection, Modena.

70. *Shells*, 1932.
Pencil on paper, 7¹/4 × 10¹/8 in.
Signed and dated lower right: Morandi
1932.
G. Salvaterra Collection, Modena.

71. *Landscape*, 1942.
Pencil on paper, 9 × 12⁵/8 in.
Signed and dated lower center: Morandi
1942.
Private collection, Rome.

72. *Still Life with Shells*, 1943.
Pencil on paper, 6¹/4 × 9 in.
Signed and dated lower right: M. 1943.
G. Domeniconi Collection, Modena.

73. *Flowers*, 1946.
Ink on paper, 11 × 7⁷/8 in.
Signed and dated lower center: Morandi
1946.
Private collection, Rome.

74. *Still Life*, 1948.
Pencil on paper, 6⁷/8 × 9⁷/8 in.
Signed and dated lower left: Morandi
1948.
Private collection, Bologna.

75. *Still Life*, 1948.
Pencil on paper, 8¹/4 × 11³/8 in.
Signed and dated lower center: Morandi
1948.
Private collection, Biella.

76. *Still Life*, 1949.
Pencil on paper, 13³/8 × 9⁷/8 in.
Signed and dated lower center: Morandi
1949.
Private collection, Bologna.

77. *Still Life*, 1953.
Pencil on paper, 6¹/2 × 9⁵/8 in.
Signed and dated lower center: Morandi
53.
Private collection, Bologna.

78. *Still Life*, 1958.
Pencil on paper, 6¹/2 × 9¹/2 in.
Signed and dated lower left: Morandi
1958.
Private collection, Bologna.

79. *Landscape*, n.d. (1960).
Pencil on paper, 9¹/2 × 13 in.
Signed lower right: Morandi.
Private collection, Bologna.

80. *Landscape*, 1962.
Pencil on paper, 8⁷/8 × 6¹/8 in.
Signed and dated lower center: Morandi /
1962.
G. Domeniconi Collection, Modena.

81. *Flowers*, n.d. (1963).
Pencil on paper, 9¹/₂ × 6¹/₂ in.
Signed lower center: Morandi.
Private collection, Bologna.

Etchings

82. *Landscape - Grizzana*, 1913.
Etching on zinc, 6³/₈ × 9¹/₄ in.
Galleria Comunale d'Arte Moderna,
Bologna.

83. *Still Life with Vase, Shells and Guitar*,
1921.
Etching on copper, 4 × 4⁵/₈ in.
Galleria Comunale d'Arte Moderna,
Bologna.

84. *Tennis Court in the Margherita Gardens
in Bologna* (small plate), 1921.
Etching on zinc, 4¹/₂ × 5³/₈ in.
Galleria Comunale d'Arte Moderna,
Bologna.

85. *Still Life with Sugar Bowl, Lemon and
Bread*, 1921 or 1922.
Etching on copper, 3¹/₄ × 4 in.
Galleria Comunale d'Arte Moderna,
Bologna.

86. *Tennis Court in the Margherita Gardens
in Bologna* (large plate), 1923.
Etching on zinc, 6³/₈ × 8¹/₈ in.
Galleria Comunale d'Arte Moderna,
Bologna.

87. *Landscape of Chiesanuova*, 1924.
Etching on copper, 6¹/₄ × 6¹/₈ in.
Galleria Comunale d'Arte Moderna,
Bologna.

88. *Cornet of Wild Flowers*, 1924.
Etching on zinc, 8¹/₈ × 6³/₈ in.
Galleria Comunale d'Arte Moderna,
Bologna.

89. *Striped Vase with Flowers*, 1924.
Etching on zinc, 9¹/₄ × 7⁷/₈ in.
Galleria Comunale d'Arte Moderna,
Bologna.

90. *The Garden of Via Fondazza*, 1924.
Etching on zinc, 4¹/₄ × 6 in.
Galleria Comunale d'Arte Moderna,
Bologna.

91. *Landscape over the Poggio*, 1927.
Etching on copper, 9¹/₄ × 11³/₈ in.
Galleria Comunale d'Arte Moderna,
Bologna.

92. *Landscape with Tall Poplar*, 1927.
Etching on copper, 12³/₄ × 9¹/₄ in.
Galleria Comunale d'Arte Moderna,
Bologna.

93. *Still Life with Pears and Grapes*, 1927.
Etching on copper, 7¹/₄ × 8¹/₄ in.
Galleria Comunale d'Arte Moderna,
Bologna.

94. *Flowers in a Small White Vase*, 1928.
Etching on zinc, 9⁵/₈ × 6³/₈ in.
Private collection, Bologna.

95. *Landscape (Plain of Bologna)*, 1929.
Etching on zinc, 9³/₄ × 11⁷/₈ in.
Galleria Comunale d'Arte Moderna, Bologna.

96. *Haystack at Grizzana*, 1929.
Etching on zinc, 9³/₄ × 10¹/₈ in.
Galleria Comunale d'Arte Moderna,
Bologna.

97. *Flowers in a Cornet on Oval-Shaped
Background*, 1929.
Etching on copper, 11⁵/₈ × 7³/₄ in.
Galleria Comunale d'Arte Moderna,
Bologna.

98. *Still Life*, 1930.
Etching on copper, 9³/₈ × 11³/₈ in.
Galleria Comunale d'Arte Moderna,
Bologna.

99. *Still Life with Cloth*, 1931.
Etching on copper, 9³/₄ × 12³/₈ in.
Galleria Comunale d'Arte Moderna,
Bologna.

100. *Still Life with White Objects on Dark
Background*, 1931.
Etching on copper, 9⁵/₈ × 11³/₈ in.
Galleria Comunale d'Arte Moderna,
Bologna.

101. *Group of Zinnias*, 1931.
Etching on zinc, 9 × 7¹/₂ in.
Galleria Comunale d'Arte Moderna,
Bologna.

102. *Zinnias in a Vase*, 1932.

Etching on zinc, 8 × 7⁵/₈ in.
Galleria Comunale d'Arte Moderna,
Bologna.

103. *View of the Montagnola in Bologna*,
1932.
Etching on copper, 8¹/₄ × 12⁷/₈ in.
Galleria Comunale d'Arte Moderna,
Bologna.

104. *Landscape of Grizzana*, 1932.
Etching on copper, 7⁷/₈ × 7 in.
Galleria Comunale d'Arte Moderna,
Bologna.

105. *Still Life*, 1933.
Etching on copper, 10¹/₈ × 12 in.
Galleria Comunale d'Arte Moderna,
Bologna.

106. *Still Life in Fine Lines*, 1933.
Etching on copper, 9⁷/₈ × 9¹/₄ in.
Galleria Comunale d'Arte Moderna,
Bologna.

107. *Large Dark Still Life*, 1934.
Etching on copper, 11⁵/₈ × 15¹/₈ in.
Galleria Comunale d'Arte Moderna,
Bologna.

108. *Large Circular Still Life with Bottle and
Three Objects*, 1946.
Etching on copper, 12³/₄ × 10¹/₈ in.
Galleria Comunale d'Arte Moderna,
Bologna.

109. *Still Life with Nine Objects*, 1954.
Etching on copper, 7¹/₈ × 9⁷/₈ in.
Galleria Comunale d'Arte Moderna,
Bologna.

110. *Still Life with Five Objects*, 1956.
Etching on copper, 5¹/₂ × 7⁷/₈ in.
Galleria Comunale d'Arte Moderna,
Bologna.

111. *Small Still Life with Three Objects*,
1961.
Etching on copper, 4⁷/₈ × 6¹/₄ in.
Galleria Comunale d'Arte Moderna,
Bologna.

112. *Still Life with Seven Objects in a Tondo*, 1945.
Etching on copper, 10¹/₂ × 11³/₄ in.
Galleria Comunale d'Arte Moderna,
Bologna.

Finito di stampare nel mese di luglio 1988
presso la Leva spa Arti Grafiche di Sesto S. Giovanni (MI)
per conto delle Nuove Edizioni Gabriele Mazzotta srl